Meditations
from
Kierkegaard

Meditations
from
Kierkegaard

Søren Aabye ...

Translated and Edited by
T. H. CROXALL

Philadelphia
THE WESTMINSTER PRESS

Library of Congress Catalog Card Number: 55–8596

PRINTED IN THE UNITED STATES OF AMERICA

To My Wife,

whose Christian insight has thrown light on
many a passage; whose co-operation in
selecting and arranging the pieces has been
of inestimable value; and whose love of
Kierkegaard's teaching has grown with the
years, as she and I together have traveled
and grown with Kierkegaard

CONTENTS

Part II THE SERMON ON THE MOUNT

Part III SOME BIBLICAL PERSONALITIES

Part IV PARABLES AND MIRACLES OF JESUS

Part V GENERAL

FOREWORD

THERE IS NO GARDEN, says Kierkegaard, whose flowers are more in quantity or greater in beauty than the ever-flowering garden of a pure human mind. The truth of this is I think demonstrated, in its degree, in the following pages. These pages contain, admittedly, but a few bouquets, taken from the vast garden of Kierkegaard's mind; a garden laid out in the fourteen volumes of his Works (*Vaerker*) and the twenty volumes of his Journals and Papers (*Papirer*). But few though these selections are, they contain, I think, a wealth of beauty, fragrance, and sustenance.

It is from the largely untranslated *Papirer* that I have generally made my selections, though I could not refrain from adding a few outstandingly lovely pieces from the *Vaerker* also. In the comparatively few cases where I have used material already translated, I have in every case made my own new translation; though I give, in the references, besides the Danish source, the reference to the already existing English translation. Where there is no other English translation, the Danish reference of course stands alone. Thus all the translations, and most of the material here used, are new to the English reader.

To select these meditations out of the vast mass of material Kierkegaard gives us has been no simple task, and I admit that many other and different types of selection would have been equally possible and equally helpful. I have laid weight upon the Passion because the Gospels themselves do so; and it seemed to me right also to give a special section to the Sermon on the Mount. Though the third part is devoted to personalities, there are also of necessity some personalities — Stephen, The Holy Innocents, and (in the Passion section) Peter, Judas, Barabbas, Pilate and others — included in the part first marked "For Times and Seasons." Of course the passages in Part I may be read at any time. Kierkegaard asks us in one place, "Are you the sort of person who, punctually at the stroke of the clock, and by the date

11

of the calendar, is able to put himself into a definite mood? Or do you imagine it is Christianity's intention that we should be like that, and not rather that we should bring together the various factors in Christianity?" (XII. p. 402; FSE 85.) It is the latter that my selections, in their small way, try to do.

The selections are in the main centered around the New Testament, though there are also some connected with the Old Testament, especially perhaps in Part III. I have there given no less than three Meditations on Abraham, because that Patriarch figures so forcibly in Kierkegaard's thought, notably in his book *Fear and Trembling*. Job is another important figure in Kierkegaard, notably in his book *Repetition*, so I have allotted two Meditations to him.

I have grouped my selections, which are mostly smaller pieces, according to a definite plan. A passage of Scripture is first given (selected where necessary by myself), around which the readings move. Then follow the selections from Kierkegaard himself, usually including a prayer, always from Kierkegaard's own pen.

Entries in the *Papirer* are of course in the nature of notes and jottings, often very compressed and epigrammatic, rough and ready. Sometimes therefore — though always with the utmost possible care not to change one iota of the sense — I have expanded or adapted these entries; though generally I have tried to leave them as they are. I have myself long found the *Papirer* invaluable for devotional reading, and over and over again, by a little adaptation, I have been able to turn a thought from Kierkegaard into a prayer for myself. Such adaptation I have occasionally found helpful in the following pages, always indicating this in the references as "adapted," or by enclosing my own amplifications in brackets [ ]. The prayers here given are for use as *private* prayers, prayers in which the soul speaks with the entire intimacy of a child speaking with his father. But of course it is open to any reader to substitute or add his own prayers.

Besides offering new translations, there is another sense in which my selection is "new"; I mean in its form and presentation. Sören Kierkegaard is a deep philosopher, but he is first and foremost a Christian; a penetrating student and exponent of the Scriptures; and, above all, a man of prayer and meditation, who, as he himself confesses, spent time every day in the quiet of his chamber with God. (Cf. X⁴. A. 195; II. A. 730.) This last is what he wants us to do too. He does not, so he often tells us, wish us to address the world at large, in general and objective terms, such as philosophers use. Rather, he seeks "that individual," "the individual, every individual, or everyone as an individual," who, in the quietness of his heart, will listen to a message that is personal and subjective, not general and objective. In a word, he seeks a reader who will appropriate the meaning and implications of Christianity for himself. But he only ventures to address others after addressing himself. "When each individual does as I have done when I write, shuts his door, reads for himself, fully conscious that I have not — and this indeed is true — in the remotest way wanted to take liberties with him, or speak to others about him, since I have thought only about myself — then truly I need not fear that he will be angry with me for what I say." (XII. p. 431; JY 109.)

It is in this spirit I too would offer my little book — which after all is not mine but Kierkegaard's. My invitation to myself first, and then my reader, is that each of us shut his door, each regard himself, like Kierkegaard before us, as an "individual before God," each read slowly and prayerfully. Then, and not by the multitudinous subtleties of philosophy, we shall come to the heart of God. To read aright we need a conscience, not only a mind. "For what is it, to be, and will to be, the individual? It is to have, and will to have, a conscience." (*Ibid.*)

I beg the reader to use these Meditations unhurriedly. Why, Kierkegaard constantly asks, are we in such a hurry? Kierkegaard's thought is often so original and arresting that to grasp its full implications may require more than one reading. Only with patience can the seed falling from Kierkegaard's flowers get time to take root in the soul, and blossom there as he would have it do.

Let me close by translating a passage from the preface to the first religious work Kierkegaard ever wrote. I would fain it stood as the Foreword here. "I have not," he says, "taken leave of this little book without an almost fanciful hope. Since the book, in being published, is, in a figurative sense, starting out on a kind of journey, I let my eye follow it for a little while. I saw how it went its way down lonely paths, or lonely along dangerous highways. After a few little misunderstandings, due to its being deceived by this or that fleeting resemblance to what it sought, it finally met 'that individual' whom with joy and gratitude I call *my* reader; 'that individual' whom it seeks, and toward whom it as it were stretches out its arms; 'that individual' who is willing enough to let himself be found, willing enough to let himself receive it, whether at the moment of meeting the book he was happy and confident or 'weary and worn and sad.' [1]

"But since on the other hand, the book, in being published, remains, in a literal sense, quite still, and does not leave its place, I let my eye rest upon it for a little while. It stood there, like an insignificant little blossom, in the shelter of a great wood, sought neither for its splendor nor for its fragrance, nor for its sustenance. But I saw also, or thought I saw, how the bird whom I call *my* reader flew down upon the wing, plucked it off, and took it to himself. And when I had seen this, I saw no more." (III. p. 15; ED I. p. 5.)

[1] Literally "weary and thoughtful." It is a well-known Danish quotation, so I have substituted a well-known English one.

ACKNOWLEDGMENTS AND REFERENCES

I DESIRE to express my deep gratitude to Frøken Kirsten Bruun, for kindly checking my translation, typing, and often retyping, the sheets, and being at great pains to help me in all respects to accuracy. And I thank Miss Catherine Højgaard too, who on not a few occasions has rendered me similar service. I owe deep gratitude to Dr. Paul Minear, who with Christian magnanimity has backed my project from the start, and has undertaken the arduous task of making the final arrangements for the printing of the manuscript.

As for the references, a letter in the middle of a reference (e.g., II. C. 24) indicates the latest edition of the *Papirer*, and the last figure, whether in the Danish original or the English translation (Dru's *Journals*), indicates, not a page, but the number of the entry. A reference with no letter in the middle (e.g., II. p. 24) indicates that it is from the *Vaerker*, and the last figure refers to a page. In Nicodemus I, the letters E.P. denote the *first* edition of the *Papirer*, which are entitled *Efterladte Papirer*. Existing English translations are identified with abbreviations.

The following abbreviations are used:

ab — abridged.

ad — adapted.

CD — *Christian Discourses*, trans. by W. Lowrie. Oxford University Press, 1939.

CL — *Consider the Lilies* (being Part II of *Edifying Discourses in a Different Vein*), trans. by A. S. Aldworth and W. S. Ferrie. The C. W. Daniel Company, Ltd., 1940.[1]

CUP — *Concluding Unscientific Postscript*, by D. F. Swenson

[1] Also trans. by D. F. and L. M. Swenson along with *Gospel of Suffering*, under the title *What We Learn from the Lilies of the Field*.

15

and W. Lowrie. Oxford University Press; Princeton University Press, 1941.

ED — *Edifying Discourses*, 4 vols., trans. by D. F. Swenson and L. M. Swenson. Augsburg Publishing House, 1943–1946.

EO — *Either/Or*, 2 vols. Vol. I trans. by D. F. and L. M. Swenson; Vol. II by W. Lowrie. Princeton University Press, 1944; Oxford University Press, 1945.

FSE — *For Self-examination*, and *Judge for Yourselves!*, and *Two Discourses at Communion*, trans. by W. Lowrie. Oxford University Press, 1941. Also *An Edifying Discourse*, trans. by D. F. Swenson. Princeton University Press, 1944.

FT — *Fear and Trembling*, trans. by W. Lowrie. Princeton University, 1941.[1]

GS — *Gospel of Suffering* (being Part II of *Edifying Discourses in a Different Vein*) and *What We Learn from the Lilies of the Field*, trans. by D. F. and L. M. Swenson. Augsburg Publishing House, 1948.

J — *Journals, A Selection*, trans. by A. Dru. Oxford University Press, 1938.

JY — *Judge for Yourselves!* See FSE above.

PA — *The Present Age*, trans. by A. Dru and W. Lowrie. Oxford University Press, 1940.

PF — *Philosophical Fragments*, trans. by D. F. Swenson. Oxford University Press, 1936; Princeton University Press, 1944.

PH — *Purify Your Hearts* (being Part I of *Edifying Discourses in a Different Vein*), trans. by A. S. Aldworth and W. S. Ferrie. The C. W. Daniel Company, Ltd., 1938.[2]

R — *Repetition*, trans. by W. Lowrie. Princeton University Press, 1941; Oxford University Press, 1942.

[1] Also trans. by R. Paine. Oxford University Press, 1939.
[2] Also trans. by D. V. Steere, Harper & Brothers, 1938, under the title *Purity of Heart*.

S   — *Stages on Life's Way,* trans. by W. Lowrie. Oxford University Press; Princeton University Press, 1940.

SD — *Sickness Unto Death,* trans. by W. Lowrie. Princeton University Press, 1941; Oxford University Press, 1941.

TC — *Training in Christianity,* and *The Woman That Was a Sinner,* trans. by W. Lowrie. Oxford University Press, 1941; Princeton University Press, 1944.

TCS — *Thoughts on Crucial Situations in Human Life,* trans. by D. F. Swenson. Augsburg Publishing House, 1941.

WL — *Works of Love,* trans. by D. F. and L. M. Swenson. Princeton University Press, 1946.

PRELIMINARY MEDITATION

ON READING THE SCRIPTURES

*All Scripture is given by inspiration of God, and is profitable
for doctrine, for reproof, for correction, for instruction in righteousness. (II Tim. 3:16.)*

*For whatsoever things were written aforetime were written for
our learning, that we through patience and comfort of the Scriptures might have hope. (Rom. 15:4.)*

TWO FIRST AND LAST THOUGHTS
1. Holy Scripture is the Signpost, the Directory. Christ is the
Way. [VIII. A. 50.]
2. Christ is the life of Holy Scripture. He was certain that what
he suffered made satisfaction for all and he had the comfort that
at his every step, and by his every word " the Scripture was fulfilled." [X¹. A. 587.]

HOW THE NEW TESTAMENT'S SOLE DESIRE IS TO CAPTURE THOSE
WHO READ IT
The fundamental way Christianity has been confounded is,
as I have said often enough, to turn it into doctrine. When studying a doctrine, we must first and foremost take the fullest possible care to study it all. With the New Testament the opposite
is the case. Its concern is with conduct, and therefore it wants
you quite simply to begin by taking a single point, and then see
that you act upon it. What a man *has* to do is always easy to understand; so easy that the most stupid person can understand it

19

immediately. If we had to act according to profundity, then God would be but a sorry sort of lawgiver, who, presumably to enjoy the fact that his laws could not be kept, made them so profound that men had to spend their lives in interpreting them; and so were rather to be excused if they did not get time to fulfill them, or even to begin on them, because right up to their last moment it had not become clear to them what the law required. [X³. A. 169.]

There is something we ought always to keep before our eyes when reading Holy Scripture, that however much we stress the resolute steadfastness of attitude which characterizes the lives of the sacred writers, emotion also had its rightful influence and exercised it. Remembering this, we shall not doubt that we possess, however remotely, some likeness to these men of God, whose countenances were transfigured by the glory of their unparalleled victories over the world. On the other hand, the deep sorrows and awful struggles in our souls are bound to make us wholly mistrust our strength to bear what it falls to our lot to bear. But if, when we are in either of these moods, we recall that there have been light as well as dark patches in our own past experience, we shall not lose our balance; and we shall neither imagine that results are achieved all at once nor despair when we realize this fact. [II. A. 479.]

OUR MODERN WAY OF READING THE NEW TESTAMENT

Imagine one of the ancient fathers of the Church, and let him be witness of the way we read the New Testament. We pass over all that concerns our lives; we omit it literally as though it were not there. That is what we do, literally. The ancients took quite literally what they read.

But I am this much nearer to the ancient fathers than is the average modern man, that at least I admit and concede what stands in the New Testament. I cannot really go further than that. My progress is paralyzed by the current illusion that we are all Christians. But at least I am like an outcry, an outcry of conscience as to where we stand. To do more would require authority,[1] because one would really have to give a fundamental definition of what it is to be a Christian. [X⁴. A. 122.]

In a Sermon on the Gospel for Easter Monday, Luther closes by making this distinction. He says: "In relation to the *Bible* you are allowed to argue. In relationship to *Holy Scripture,* you are not." This is a new edition of the old saying, "A thing may be true in philosophy which is not true in theology." [2]

The Bible and Holy Scripture are indeed the same book but the way in which we deal with them makes the difference.

Here, as everywhere, we must pay heed to the qualitative leap, and realize that there is no direct transition from reading and studying the Bible as an ordinary human book to accepting it as God's word and sacred writing. There is a leap into another territory, whereby I break off from chains of reasoning, and accept in Holy Scripture something quite new in quality, something of quite another order. [X¹. A. 361.]

PRAYER

Only in frail earthen vessels do we men carry what is sacred. But thou, O Holy Spirit, when thou dwellest in man, dost dwell in what is of infinitely smaller worth than that. Spirit of holiness, thou dwellest in impurity and pollution. Spirit of wisdom, thou dwellest in foolishness. Spirit of truth, thou dwellest in self-deceit. O continue to dwell with us, thou who dost not seek the comfort of a pleasant dwelling place, which indeed thou wouldst seek in vain. Thou who by creating and giving new birth dost make for thyself thy dwelling, O continue to dwell with us. And may it so end that thou findest pleasure in the dwelling which thou hast prepared for thyself in my polluted, foolish, and self-deceived heart. [X². A. 344.]

[1] Kierkegaard insists that, not being an ordained priest, he was "without authority," uttering his strictures and his teaching as a private person.
[2] This was the so-called Alexandrine teaching of the fifteenth century, which was condemned by the Catholic Church.

PART

I

FOR TIMES AND SEASONS

"PREPARE YE THE WAY OF THE LORD"

In those days came John the Baptist, preaching in the wilderness of Judea. (Matt. 3:1.)

And as they departed, Jesus began to say unto the multitudes concerning John, What went ye out into the wilderness to see? A reed shaken with the wind? But what went ye out for to see? A man clothed in soft raiment? behold, they that wear soft clothing are in kings' houses. But what went ye out for to see? A prophet? yea, I say unto you, and more than a prophet. For this is he, of whom it is written, Behold, I send my messenger before thy face, which shall prepare thy way before thee. (Matt. 11:7–10.)

PRAYER BEFORE THE SERMON

Father in heaven, our thoughts turn to thee. They seek thee again in this hour, not as with the faltering step of an erring wanderer, but with the sure flight of the homing bird. Let not our trust in thee be but a fleeting thought, or a mometary impulse, or the delusive calm of an earth-bound heart. Let not our longings for thy Kingdom, our expectations of thy glory, be fruitless sighings, or like waterless clouds. But let them be lifted up to thee from our full hearts, and granted as the refreshing dew which moistens our tongues, and as thy heavenly manna which feeds us forever! [II. A. 285.]

SKETCH OF SERMON

Devout hearers! What went ye out into the wilderness to see? This is the serious preparative question wherewith John, as the Lord's forerunner, prepares the way of the Lord in people's minds, and invites the Jews to reflect upon. We also may sometimes be tempted to ask the same question when we come to this holy place to proclaim the Word.

(*a*) What have *you* come out to see? Was it *a person clothed in fine raiment?* Was it a discourse you would hear, decked out in

25

human fashion with earthly pomp and glory? Seek it in your own assemblies. And were I foolish enough to attempt that kind of discourse, I would wish that I might in the end amass a power like Samson's to overthrow the temple's glory (which I, like him, have no eye for), even if it were to my own destruction.

(*b*) Was it *a reed that was shaken hither and thither in the wind?* Was it a discourse designed to aid the daydreams of the sluggish, and to lull those who are awake into sleep? Seek it in the streets and market places. But truly, such a discourse is (as many a person wants it to be) swayed by the wind; therefore it shall be wafted away like chaff before the winnowing fan which the Lord has in his hand.

(*c*) No, my discourse shall be as the wild honey — its clothing as the wild raiment wherewith John the Baptist was clothed. It shall be rugged and sharp; to many perhaps a hard speech. Yet thou, O God, dwellest not in temples made with hands — still less dost thou make thy dwelling in elegant phrases. [II. A. 286.]

"THIS DAY . . . A SAVIOUR"

Unto you is born this day . . . a Saviour. (Luke 2:11.)

"Today." And yet it was night when he was born. This is an eternal picture. Without Christ, night in the soul is inevitable; and yet it becomes day in the middle of that night, when the Saviour is born.

"Today." This is an eternal date, just as it is when God says "today," [1] and, like the books which come out "this year," this "today" is repeated from generation to generation, for every individual in all the millions that are born. And every time someone truly becomes a Christian, it means, — "Unto *you* is born this day a Saviour." [X². A. 283; J 1019.]

[1] Cf. Ps. 95:7; Heb. 3:13.

Christ's birth is not only an event on earth but also in heaven. Our justification is likewise not only an event on earth but also in heaven. [II. A. 594; J 104.]

Christ is for all time as much God as man. Think of the sea; the sky appears just as deeply in it as heaven is high above it. [II. A. 595.]

When Christ decided to become the world's Saviour, there went as it were a sigh through all mankind, saying: " Why do you do this? You make us all unhappy." For indeed to become a true Christian involves the greatest human suffering; for Christ the Absolute breaks down all the relativity in which we men live, in order to make us spiritual beings. But in order to become spiritual we have to go through crises which make us, humanly speaking, as unhappy as possible. It might be objected to this, " On the contrary, at Christ's birth, a song of *joy* was heard from the angels." To which it might be answered, " But it is angels who sing, not men." To this again it may be answered: " But take the word ' Saviour,' and let people define what is to be understood by that word. We shall not wonder then if men rejoice."

But all this is to take Christianity in vain. When we come to define the word " Saviour " more closely, the idea of God presents itself, and that idea Christ absolutely fulfills. In him we find it exemplified once more that for a man, humanly speaking, it is the greatest suffering to be a Christian. To be saved means just this.

Luther rightly says in a sermon on the Gospel for Christmas Day, that there is nothing to be said of Christ but that he is " a great joy." But only " for sin-bruised hearts," he says. Otherwise not; for otherwise we take Christ in vain. [X³. A. 526.]

PRAYER

O Lord Jesus Christ, would that we might see thee in thy true form; that we might see thee as thou art and wast and wilt be till thy coming again in glory; see thee as the sign of offense and the object of faith; the lowly man and yet the Saviour and Redeemer of our race, who out of love came to earth in order to seek the lost. [XII. p. 19 f. ab; TC p. 9.]

STEPHEN

And all that sat in the council, looking steadfastly on him, saw his face as it had been the face of an angel. (Acts 6:15.)

And they stoned Stephen, calling upon God, and saying, Lord Jesus, receive my spirit. And he kneeled down, and cried with a loud voice, Lord, lay not this sin to their charge. And when he had said this, he fell asleep. (Acts 7:59, 60.)

THEME: GOD'S KINGDOM IS NOT OF THIS WORLD

St. Stephen's Day, December 26, contains a further explication of the meaning of Christmas Day. It tells us for what purpose Christ was born, viz., in order that the natural man in him should die.

In so-called Christendom we in Denmark have made Christmas into *the* great festival. This is quite false, and was not at all so in the Early Church. We mistake childishness for Christianity — that is what all our sickly sentimentality, with pepper nuts [1] and the Christmas babe, comes to.

" They saw the face of Stephen as it had been the face of an angel." In our human speech we often say of a child that he looks like an angel. Christianly speaking, a dying man does. To die is to be born again. [VIII. A. 470.]

" When he had said this he fell asleep." Surely a man ought to be able to sleep easily when he has prayed for his enemies. [VIII. A. 475.]

[1] A sweetmeat eaten at Christmas in Denmark.

When a man is at the point of death, he has a lot of things to see to before he dies, such as bequeathing a will, etc. After that, he turns over and dies. Stephen also had something to see to. He must first pray for his enemies, and when that was done, he died. He really bequeathed nothing, because nobody would receive his intercessions for them. So he took them also with him. [VIII. A. 546.]

Christ in his glory is not indifferent or inactive. He is always ready to intercede for us with groanings that cannot be uttered. He never sits down, for when danger is great, he rises up, as Stephen saw him. [VIII. A. 374.]

"When he had said this, he fell asleep."

1. He fell asleep. How quiet! But to sleep quietly, that is the very symbol of all stillness. How quiet! Doubly quiet compared with its opposite. While the raging mob snorts out violence and murder, he — he sleeps; just as his Lord and Master slept in the boat while the storm raged. The disciple here imitated his Master. He slept while *this* storm raged.

2. "He fell asleep." How mighty — or, seen from the other side, how weak art thou, thou ungodly world! How weak in all thy raging and tumult! What can you do? Lo, this is what you do; he sleeps! Be sleepless in your exasperation. Be able to upset everything — but you cannot upset him, nor any sleeper like him. How mighty to be able to sleep at the crucial moment; and not only to be able to sleep at such a moment, but to get off to sleep at such a moment! How little it usually takes to disturb a person's sleep — but thus to be able to sleep! . . . Fast bound art thou to laughter, O world, with thy weakness: he sleeps, he sleeps from it all. He does not strive against thee. No, far from it, he sleeps. He answers thee not. No, far from it, he sleeps. He has nothing to do with thee. No, far from it, he sleeps. So far is he from thee; far away, absent. He sleeps.

3. "*When he had said this,* he fell asleep." What was it he said? He said, "Father, lay not this sin to their charge." This therefore

is the formula — then we may fall asleep. As one tells a child to read a prayer aloud and then go to sleep, so slept he; or, rather, "when he had said *this*." He prayed for them. For himself he had prayed again and again. His whole life until the last, his sufferings — in all this he had prayed for himself. Now there is only a moment left, one minute. He prays for his enemies. Yet one must confess that the shorter our allotted time is, the easier it perhaps is to decide to pray for one's enemies. If he had had to live longer with them, it would perhaps not have been so easy to pray for them.

But we learn of him to pray for ourselves and to pray for our enemies. Then we may fall asleep. Sleep on then, sleep sweetly! For nineteen hundred years Stephen has been extolled and praised. But it troubles him so little — he sleeps. [X⁴. A. 434.]

What is asked of a man that he may be able to pray for his ene-mies? To pray for one's enemies is the hardest thing of all. That is why it exasperates us so much in our present-day situation. [X⁴. A. 435.]

When the world shuts itself against a man, heaven opens for him. The animals do not see heaven. The upright heathen did see heaven. But heaven opened — that only the Christian sees, and especially the martyr. Against him the world shuts itself in the strongest possible measure. [X⁴. A. 436.]

Christmastide begins and ends with angels. Yesterday angels announced that a Saviour is born. Today Stephen bears witness to this fact, and they saw his face as it had been the face of an angel. Someone will say: "Angels? Nobody has ever seen angels. That is something for children." Answer: "Stuff and nonsense! Hold your tongue! Only see to it that you become like Stephen, that your face is as an angel's face — then we others have an angel to look at." [X⁴. A. 438.]

THE HOLY INNOCENTS

Then Herod, when he saw that he was mocked of the wise men, was exceeding wroth, and sent forth, and slew all the children that were in Bethlehem, and in all the coasts thereof, from two years old and under. (Matt. 2:16.)

John answered and said, . . . He must increase, but I must decrease. (John 3:27, 30.)

Christ was born in a stable, wrapped in swaddling clothes, and laid in a manger: so insignificant is this child in appearance, so meanly conditioned. But ere long he becomes so precious that it costs the children in Bethlehem their lives. Such is the possible lavishness where this child is concerned. [X². A. 38.]

Imagine a man who could not help seeing that a new day was beginning to dawn; that his sun of success was beginning to decline, and another was the favored one; (for it is not the concern of Truth to be successful). His soul, let us imagine, was unacquainted with humility and self-negation; he could not bear it that a new Pharaoh has ascended the throne who knew not Joseph. So like Herod he commanded that all children under two years of age should be slain. Or he hid himself, and abandoned himself to grief, as if only that man " increased " who was planted by the waterside (Ps. 1:3), and not he also who plants himself in the blessed soil of self-negation.

Ah, how many ways there are to take in the hour of decision! And yet there is only one true way; the others are deviations, which lead either to where envy lays its plans, or where repining has its home; where the worm of desire dies not; where desolation stares at its loss; where ridicule pains others by its paltry philosophy; where the tongue of malice betrays how full the heart is. Thought dare not even follow them. But humble self-negation remains true to itself, and continues in full understanding with the one who must increase, as John did. For when John testified saying, " I must decrease," his sun went down. And yet when was he greater than at that moment? For in fact he increased, and was greatest when he (like the sun) went down. [IV. p. 188 ad; ED III. p. 132.]

PRAYER

Grant Lord that with humble self-denial and sincere joy, I may see others increase, and my heart be turned to a new joy; and may this my new joy be fulfilled. [IV. p. 193 f.; ED III. p. 139.]

GOD'S VICTORY IN HUMILIATION

Though he was divine by nature, he did not set store upon equality with God, but emptied himself by taking the nature of a servant; born in human guise and appearing in human form, he humbly stooped in his obedience even to die, and to die upon the cross. (Phil. 2:6–8, Moffatt.)

Suppose there was a king who loved a humble maiden. The king's heart was not affected by that wisdom which is so loudly preached; he was unacquainted with those difficulties which the intellect discovers in order to constrain the heart: difficulties which give the poets plenty to do, and make their magic formulas necessary. His resolve was easy to carry out, because all his councilors feared his wrath, and dared not breathe a word. All the foreign states too trembled before his power and dared not omit to send ambassadors with good wishes for the nuptials. Cringing courtiers groveling in the dust dared not wound him, lest their own heads should be crushed. Let then the harp be tuned. Let the songs of the poets begin. Let all be festive, while love celebrates

its triumph. For love is exultant when it unites equals, but tri-
umphant when it makes equal in love that which before was un-
equal.[1]

But then there awoke a qualm in the soul of the king. Who
would have dreamed of such a thing except a king with kingly
thoughts! He spoke to no one about his qualms, for had he done
so, each courtier would doubtless have said, " Your Majesty, you
do a good deed toward the girl, for which she will not be able to
thank you enough all her life." This would doubtless have aroused
the king's wrath against the courtier, so that he would have had
him executed for high treason against the king's beloved. And
that would have caused sorrow to the king in another way. Alone
therefore he wrestled with the sorrow in his heart. Would the
maiden be happy? Would she gain sufficient self-confidence never
to recall what the king wished only to forget, namely, that he was
a king, and she had been a lowly maiden? For if this happened; if
the memory of her former lowliness awoke within her, and at
times, like a favored rival, stole her thoughts away from the king,
alluring her reflection unto the seclusion of a secret grief; or if this
memory at times crossed her soul like death crossing over a grave
— where then would be the glory of their love? She would have
been happier had she remained in her obscurity, loved by an
equal, content in her little cottage, but quite at ease in her love,
and cheerful, early and late. What a rich abundance of sorrow
stands ripe, so to say, almost weighed down by the weight of its
own fruitfulness, only awaiting the harvest, when the king's
thoughts must thresh out all its seed of sorrow!

And even if the maiden were content to become as nothing,
the king could not be satisfied, just because he loved her. He
would rather lose her than be her benefactor.

Or suppose she could not understand him (for as we are speaking foolishly about human affairs, we can imagine a difference of

---

[1] Kierkegaard is thinking respectively of the *ovatio* and the *triumphus*
in Rome. The *ovatio* was accorded for bloodless victories or victories
over slaves. The general accorded the *ovatio* entered the city on horse-
back only. In the *triumphus*, accorded for greater victories, he rode in
a chariot.

mind between them which makes understanding impossible). What deep sorrow there would be, slumbering in this unhappy love! Who would dare to rouse it?

The disciple is in error through his own fault. Yet he is the object of love to the God I am depicting. This God desires to teach him, and so is concerned to make him equal with himself. If this equality cannot be established, love becomes unhappy, and his teaching meaningless, since they cannot understand one another.

Unity might be brought about by the elevation of the disciple. The God would then lift the disciple up to his own estate. But that unselfish king could perceive the difficulty of such a method. He knew that the maiden would really be deceived, and that in the most terrible of all ways. For no deceit is so bad as when it is unsuspected; when a person is, as it were, bewitched by a change of clothing.

Unity might be brought about by this God appearing to the disciple and receiving his worship, making the disciple forget himself thereby. In the same way the king could have appeared to the humble maiden in all his glory, making her forget herself in worshiping adoration. Alas! this might have satisfied the maiden, but it could not satisfy the king, who desired not his own glorification but hers. She could not understand him, and that made the king's sorrow the harder; but it would have been harder still to deceive her.

Not in this way, then, could love be made happy, except perhaps in appearance; and that to the disciple and maiden only, not to the teacher and the king, whom no delusion can satisfy. Take an analogy. The God I am referring to has joy in arraying the lily in a garment more glorious than Solomon. But if there could be any question of an understanding between a flower and a king, what a sorry dilemma for the lily to be in! She would wonder when she looked upon her fine garments, whether it was on account of her raiment that the God loved her. And, whereas now she stands confident in the meadow, sporting with the wind, carefree as the gust that blows, she would then languish, and not have the courage to lift up her head.

It was the God's solicitude to prevent this. The learner owes the Teacher everything, and this is what makes it so difficult to effect an understanding. Unity cannot, as we have seen, be brought about by elevation, so it must be attempted by a descent. The God must become the equal of even the lowliest disciple. But the lowliest is one who must serve others, and the God will therefore appear in the form of a *servant*. But this servant's form is not something merely put on, like the king's beggar cloak, which, because it is only a cloak, flutters loosely, and betrays the king. It is a true form. For this is the unfathomable nature of Love, that it desires equality with the beloved; not in jest, but seriously and in truth. And this is the omnipotence of Love, deciding to be equal with the beloved, that Love can accomplish its purpose in a way that no human king can. That is why the king's assumed form of equality was in a measure deceit.

Behold where he stands — the God! Where? There; do you not see him? He is the God; and yet he has nowhere to lean his head, and he dares not lean on any man lest he cause him to be offended. . . . But the servant-form was not a thing merely put on; and therefore the God must suffer all things, endure all things, make experience of all things. He must . . . yield his spirit in death and again leave the earth. . . . O bitter cup! More bitter than wormwood is the ignominy of death for a mortal; how ignominious then for an immortal! O bitter refreshment, sourer than vinegar, to be refreshed by the misunderstanding of the beloved! O solace in affliction to suffer as one who is guilty! How then shall one suffer who is innocent! [IV. p. 220 ff. ab; PF p. 20 ff.]

NEW YEAR: THE FUTURE

This is the victory that overcometh the world, even our faith.
(I John 5:4.)

When the sailor is out upon the sea, when everything is changing about him, when the billows are born and die, then he does not stare down into the depths of the waves, for they change. He looks up to the stars: and why? Because they are faithful; as they stand now, so they stood for our fathers, and will stand for the coming generations. By what means does he then conquer the changing? Through the eternal. Through the eternal one can conquer the future, because the eternal is the basis (*Grund*) of the future; therefore through the eternal one can fathom (*udgrunde*) the future. What then is the eternal power in man? Is it faith. What is the expectation of faith? Victory, or, as the Scriptures so earnestly and so movingly teach us, it is that all things certainly work together for good to those that love God. But an expectation of the future which expects victory has already conquered the future. The believer is therefore done with the future before he begins on the present; for what one has conquered no longer has power to disturb, and this victory can only make one more vigorous for the present. [III. p. 32; ED I. p. 21 f.]

When I say, " I believe," then all too often it may not be clear to me what I really mean by that. Perhaps I am mistaken; perhaps I am only creating a mental picture of the future; perhaps I am wishing, hoping, perhaps longing for something, desiring, coveting it. Or perhaps I am certain about the future. In all this, it may seem to me that I believe, although I really do not. On the other hand if I confront myself with the question, Do you expect victory?, then every obscurity becomes more difficult. I can easily perceive that he who expects nothing does not really believe. But

I perceive too that the man who is waiting upon some particular event, or grounding his hope upon some particular thing, does not believe either. This is most important. For only he who is finished with the future can be wholly and undividedly firm in the present. But one can only be finished with the future when one has conquered it. And this is precisely what faith does. Its expectation *is* conquest. Every time therefore I catch myself not expecting victory, then I know I do not believe. And when I know that, I know what I have to do. It is not easy to believe; but the first condition for believing is to know whether I really do believe or not. We often go astray because we seek for some assurance that our expectations will be realized, instead of seeking for an assurance of faith that we believe. [III. p. 40 f.; ED I. p. 31 f.]

Today, on the first day of the year, when the thought of the future obtrudes itself upon me, I will not glut my soul with all sorts of expectations, nor split it up by imagining all sorts of things. I will collect myself together, and hale and happy, please God, I will go forth to meet the future. Let it bring what it will or may. Many expectations will be disappointed, many fulfilled. That is bound to be, as experience has taught me. But there is one expectation that will not be disappointed — experience has not taught me this, but neither has it the power to disavow it — and that is the expectation of faith. And this is VICTORY. [III. p. 41; ED I. p. 32.]

PRAYER

Father in heaven! How is a man nought without thee! How is all he knows but a broken fragment, if he knows not thee! How is all he undertakes only a half task, if thou art not the master of the building! Do thou then move those who live without God in the world that they might seek thee. Form the hearts of those who seek thee that they might wait for thee. For well do we know that all seeking has its promise. Why then not the seeking that seeks thee? But we know also that all seeking has its pain, and so too does the seeking that seeks thee. Well do we know that to seek does not mean that a man must go into the wide world; for the more glorious the thing he seeks, the nearer to him does it lie. And if he seek thee, O Lord, thou art the nearest of all things to him. But for that very reason he perhaps has not yet found thee. So teach him to wait. Though the years pass, grant that he may wait. Though the opportune time of joy pass, grant that he may wait. Even though he lose everything that is not worth gaining, if he yet waited for thee, then he did not lose. [VI. B. 160.]

JOURNEYING

Now when Jesus was born in Bethlehem of Judea in the days of Herod the king, behold, there came wise men from the east to Jerusalem, saying, Where is he that is born King of the Jews? for we have seen his star in the east, and are come to worship him. When Herod the king had heard these things, he was troubled, and all Jerusalem with him. And when he had gathered all the chief priests and scribes of the people together, he demanded of them where Christ should be born. (Matt. 2:1–4.)

Although the scribes could say where the Messiah should be born, they remained quite unperturbed in Jerusalem. They did not accompany the Wise Men to seek him. Similarly a man may know the whole of Christianity, yet make no *movement*. The power that moved heaven and earth moves him not at all.

What a difference! The three kings had only a rumor to go by. But it moved them to make that long journey. The scribes were much better informed. They sat and studied the Scriptures like so many dons, but it did not make them move. Who had the more truth? The three kings who followed a rumor, or the scribes who remained sitting with all their knowledge?

What a vexation it must have been for the kings, that the scribes who gave them the news they wanted remained quiet in

Jerusalem! We are being mocked, the kings might have thought. For indeed it is a serious self-contradiction that the scribes should have the knowledge and yet remain still. It is just as serious as if a person knows about Christianity, and his own life expresses the opposite. We are tempted to suppose that he wishes to befool us, unless we admit that he is only befooling himself. [X³. A. 202.]

By faith Abraham went out from the land of his fathers and became a sojourner in the land of promise. He left one thing behind, and took one thing with him. He left his earthly understanding behind and took faith with him. Otherwise he would not have gone forth, but would have thought, This is utterly unreasonable. [III. p. 80; FT p. 20.]

Abraham is an eternal pattern of religion. As he had to go forth from the land of his fathers into a strange land, so must the man of religion go forth, leaving all his contemporaries and fellow men although he remains among them. He remains; but he is isolated, a *stranger* to them. To be a stranger and in exile is the peculiar suffering of religion. [X³. A. 114.]

GOD'S LIGHT PENETRATES OUR SECRET BEING

When they saw the star, they rejoiced with exceeding great joy. And when they were come into the house, they saw the young child with Mary his mother, and fell down, and worshipped him: and when they had opened their treasures, they presented unto him gifts; gold, and frankincense, and myrrh. (Matt. 2:10, 11.)

The glory of heaven shines over Christ's birth. It is not the case here, as at other times, that the stars of the night shine unchanged over the earth. No, his birth — which certainly seemed to be of no importance here on earth — was of importance in heaven, indeed of the greatest importance. And one star shines specially over the town where he was born, diffusing — blessed the eye that sees it — the splendor of heaven over the stable, over the despised maiden and her embarrassed husband, and over the babe in the manger. This glory of Christ is a superhuman glory. But, as always, Christianity brings opposites together, and so the glory is not to be recognized directly as glory, but, on the contrary, it is seen in lowliness and humiliation. [XII. p. 500; JY p. 172.]

Christian romance has certainly an Eastern quality, but it is only the three holy kings from the East who have seen its star, and then bring their *gifts*, gold, and precious frankincense. [II. A. 109.]

Just as every gift is good if it be received with thankfulness, so is every gift great when God blesses it. When we give with thankfulness, it is the blessing that feeds. And for our comfort — we, who have so little we can give — there is the gospel story of the widow with her poor gifts, but her rich blessing. [III. A. 88.]

Prayer
Father in heaven! Well do we know that thou dwellest in light and that thy being is utter clarity. But for this very reason thou art obscure to us, even in thy revelation; thou art as a secret which we cannot utter. But lo! this is our comfort, that thou seest in secret, and understandest from afar. Do thou thyself then try our hearts; and, according as is the secret which everyone's heart conceals, and according as thou dost understand it, vouchsafe also a revelation to us in proportion as we guard the secret and love thee. [IV. C. 1.]

WE ARE TEMPTED IN THE WILDERNESS

Then was Jesus led up of the Spirit into the wilderness to be tempted of the devil. (Matt. 4:1.)

Moments are bound to come, even before that last hour when no help is left upon earth, in which you feel yourself alone; in which you are "tempted in the wilderness," so that even if you shouted over the whole world, no voice would answer to comfort you — except that voice which the Old Testament has sketched so terrifyingly, the voice of the Omnipresent. (See Ps. 139:8, "If I take the wings of the morning, and remain in the uttermost parts of the sea, thou art there.") Yet this is precisely the voice that is so comforting to the Christian. [II. A. 293.]

It also occurs again later in the life of Christ, that he was tempted in loneliness — while the apostles sleep. The same thing happens to us at those times when it seems as if all to whom we might have turned are sleeping too soundly and immovably to be roused by our cares. Then it is necessary to find a higher comfort. [II. A. 294.]

It was "the evil spirit" that led Christ out into solitude in order to tempt him. From this, somebody might be disposed to conclude that it is always the evil spirit that leads a person out into solitude. There is sometimes truth in this; but to be alone is also the way to true fellowship with God. One may even say that the temptation of Christ in solitude was precisely that which developed him, if one can speak thus of him. Besides, God does, in a certain sense, dwell in solitude. But it is certain that solitude is dialectical [1]; and therefore a man rarely achieves anything who never

---

[1] I.e., a time for thinking things out.

was in solitude. In solitude we face the Absolute,[1] but also absolute danger. In society we face relativity and relative dangers; yet also, be it noted, a danger which is more than relative, the danger of missing the Absolute altogether; of never discovering that it is there, never getting our life ordered in relation to it, however far we may be from it. For while it is fanatical and arrogant for a person to want to be the Absolute, it is right we should understand that the Absolute is the measure by which we must be measured, both for our humiliation and for our incitement. For it humbles us to see how far we are from the Absolute; but that ought also to incite us, and keep us vigilant in the strife. [X[1]. A. 463.]

PRAYER

Lord, be thou near us with thy power, so that we may feel the heart's joyful assurance that thou art not far from us, but that we may live and move and have our being in thee. [II. A. 295.]

CHRIST'S TEMPTATIONS

Then was Jesus led up of the Spirit into the wilderness to be tempted of the devil. (Matt. 4:1.)

Christ's temptation is not only an ordinary human temptation; think how the edge of temptation is whetted when the one who hungers has it in his power to perform a miracle and create bread! This is something other than merely hungering. It is a superhuman pang, just at that moment to have the power of working miracles, and yet not to dare to use the power. [X[4]. A. 181.]

To desire God's aid in a forbidden, rebellious, and ungodly manner is a form of presumption. It is a blind superstition. Thus

---

[1] Or, let us say, Perfection.

the presumptuous heathen wants foolishly to add a cubit to his stature; in foolishness he wants what is denied him; in blind confidence he will risk a foolhardy act, will cast himself down from the pinnacle of the temple — and, what is more presumptuous still, he wants God to help him in it. [X. p. 84; CD p. 70.]

He in whose soul the inner man proclaims itself by concern will not be glad when fortune favors him in everything. Were he set on the top of a mountain to survey all the kingdoms of the world, and it was said to him, "All this is yours," he would first want to know who had set him there, and whom he had to thank. Thus prosperity would become an occasion to him for increasing his concern, and so would serve for him as a strengthening of the inner man. His rejoicing must therefore be quite different from that of the successful man who has no concern. For he who, when he possesses the world, is as one who possesses it not — *he* possesses the world. Otherwise the world possesses him. [III. p. 338 f. ab; ED I. p. 105.]

Have you forgotten that there was one who could ascend the highest mountain; who could survey the kingdoms and countries of the earth and say to the hungry one, " All these things will I give you *if* you will fall down and worship me"? Have you forgotten that this was the tempter? [IV. p. 47; ED II. p. 52.]

THE ANNUNCIATION

And in the sixth month the angel Gabriel was sent from God unto a city of Galilee, named Nazareth, to a virgin espoused to a man whose name was Joseph, of the house of David; and the virgin's name was Mary. And the angel came in unto her, and said, Hail, thou that art highly favored, the Lord is with thee: blessed art thou among women. (Luke 1:26–28.)

Who was ever so great in this world as that favored woman, the mother of God, the Virgin Mary?

What shall we say of her? That she was favored among women does not make her great. True, she has her babe in a wonderful way, but it went with her after the manner of women, and that season is one of dread, distress, and paradox. The angel was indeed a ministering spirit, but he was not so ready a minister as to go to the other young girls in Israel and say, " Despise not little Mary, what has happened to her is something extraordinary." No; the angel came to Mary only, and no one could understand her.

What woman, I wonder, was so insulted as Mary [by what people said of her]? And is it not true here as always that whom the Lord blesseth he curseth in the same breath? This is how Mary is to be spiritually interpreted. She is not in the least a lady who sits in state and plays with an infant god. (It upsets me even to mention such a thing. But it upsets me still more that thoughtless and shallow people have so understood her.)

Nevertheless, when she says, " Behold the handmaid of the Lord," then she *is* great; and I think it should not be difficult to explain why she became the mother of God. She is no stage " heroine," and does not need worldly admiration; any more than Abraham (who is no stage " hero ") needs our tears. They were both greater than heroes, not in the least because they were exempted from distress, and torment, and paradox, but precisely because they lived with such things. [III. p. 128; FT p. 97.]

Christianity is the " new creation." Hence Christ is born of a pure virgin; something is again created out of nothing. Hence also the Holy Spirit overshadowed Mary, just as aforetime he had brooded over the deep. [II. A. 31.]

The angel found the right person — because Mary chose the right thing.

Certainly she was the chosen one, and so her lot was already decided. But there is also an element of freedom and receptivity in her. This is what proves whether one is the right person. Had the angel not found her the kind of person she was, then she would not have been the right person.

She said, " Behold the handmaid of the Lord, be it unto me according to thy word."

We are so accustomed to hear these words that we may easily overlook their meaning, fondly imagining that in the same circumstances we should have answered in the same way.

Let us consider what she might — alas! far more naturally — have answered. It is good for us to consider the matter from a quite different point of view from the pietistic. Piety has bedecked this situation with its emotions, sometimes quite beautifully. It has, e.g., dwelt upon the thought that when the angel spoke to Mary it was as if all creation cried to Mary: " Say yes! Oh, hasten to say yes! "

But she *could* have smiled — yes, even as Sarah did. There was every bit as good reason. Or, if she was unable to smile, she might have felt abashed at being addressed like this, and pushed the salutation away from her.

Or she could have said: " This is too much for me. Spare me; it is beyond my power." And clearly the angel too thought it beyond her power. That is why the power of the Holy Ghost had to overshadow her. Yes, quite right. But to have the faith to become as nothing; to be a mere instrument as she was — that indeed is far more difficult than the uttermost exertion of one's powers could ever be. [X⁴. A. 454; J 1240.]

Honor be to the Virgin Mary! O God! When the tidings came to her: " You must live a life scorned by other girls, treated as a foolish imaginative wench, or a silly, half-mad, despicable creature, or as a loose woman, and so on; moreover you will be exposed to all kinds of other sufferings, and at last a sword will go through your heart when it will seem as if God has forsaken you: *this* is the glad tidings," oh, honor be to her, that without a moment's hesitation she could say, " Behold the handmaid of the Lord," and could sing in her Magnificat that all generations should call her blessed! O God! Lo, this is something quite different from being able to speak all possible languages perfectly, be they living or dead ones (as our educated young ladies do). This is to " speak with tongues." [1] [XI[1]. A. 40.]

CHRIST'S SUFFERINGS

For it became him, for whom are all things, and by whom are all things, in bringing many sons unto glory, to make the captain of their salvation perfect through sufferings. (Heb. 2:10.)

People have understood Christ's sufferings differently at different times. On the one hand there is the great physical pain, etc. But no doubt you have also felt that however wearing the grief of repentance is, the grief that seizes us when we suffer innocently — when we bear the consequences of others' guilt — is deeper. Such is Christ's sorrow. But in all his sufferings he was not the one to think of himself, or in the least to burden others with his sorrow — he who with great justification could have said to those who sought him, sought comfort from him, Do you not see how much I suffer, what a heavy burden rests upon my shoulders? And yet he was at all times and at every moment ready to listen to the woes and sufferings of others, in order to comfort them. [III. C. 6.]

It may be moving, and spiritually beneficial to myself, to live through the story of the Passion. For though in the main Christ's sufferings are narrated to make me tremble — that is, his sufferings are indeed an atonement, and I the sinner — yet his sufferings have also another side, whereby they plainly are a spiritual benefit to the sufferer. [VIII. A. 581.]

[1] To " speak with tongues " is Paul's phrase (I Cor. 14:5, *et alia*) for speaking things too great for human apprehension.

The sufferings of Christ cannot of course be understood intellectually, since the divine and the human must be held together in the mind, and this is possible only for faith. Intellectually we can cause our minds to pay attention, but there comes a moment when we must cry: "Now believe! Cast yourself down in adoration and believe!"

The depth of suffering is greatest because of the questionings that come when the sufferer has it in his power to avoid the suffering and yet chooses it: suffers in face of the advice of relatives and sympathizers who insist that he should give up the suffering and spare himself while he can. That is, suffering is here open to criticism, and that is enough to make one lose one's reason. When suffering is not voluntary, then I have my full powers to fight it with: and moreover everyone will be able to understand me. But voluntary suffering is debatable at two points. First, I must use my strength to compel myself to go forth into the suffering, and then I must use my strength to bear it.

Now as to Christ's suffering. As divine, he had everything in his power. Yet as human, he freely chose to suffer — all the time being able, because divine, to alter everything.

And so he says to his disciples, "All ye shall be offended because of me this night." (Matt. 26:31.) Why is it possible to be offended? Quite simply thus: either they may doubt whether Christ is, after all, the person he said he was, since he does not show himself the stronger; or he *is* what he said, in which case the whole thing is, humanly speaking, a dreadful farce, that he, God, should suffer like this. [VIII. A. 579.]

Blessed is he who is not offended in thee! Blessed is he who believes that Jesus Christ has lived here on earth, and that he was the person he said he was, the lowly man, yet God, the only begotten of the Father. Infinite sorrow when he who came to save us all, he who, as divine, had no concern to procure honor and dignity for himself (O madness and mockery of God!), but every day, every hour, every moment of his life thought only of others in infinite sorrow when he looked out over the multitudes of men and beheld everything else except faith and faith's understanding. [XII pp. 97, 100; TC pp. 79, 81.]

CHRIST'S GLANCE: PETER'S RESPONSE

And the Lord turned and looked upon Peter. (*Luke 22:61.*)

We are apt to speak depreciatively of Peter's denial, and appreciatively of his later life. But there is one thing we do not sufficiently mark — that a glance was enough for him. There is scarcely one in a million for whom, in those circumstances, a glance would be enough. As people now are, they would probably, every one of them, have thought themselves exceedingly lucky if they had, to their great self-satisfaction, *prudently* left the Master in the lurch. And if he had fixed his glance on them, every one of them would have complacently thought, I was prudent enough to seem as if I had not noticed anything. [XI[1]. A. 274.]

People are always busy winning disciples. It is of great importance (to themselves!) that they get them quickly. They hasten to use every means to this end, and they quickly reject everyone who is unwilling. God, on the other hand, gains his disciples by long-suffering. He gains them *at the very last moment.* So it comes about that while men's disciples fall away at the last moment, God's disciples stand firm.

This was precisely the case with Peter. Christ gained Peter when he denied him, i.e., at the last moment. And Peter stood firm.

A witness was needed, a witness in whose thought the Crucified and Risen One could linger night and day. Such a witness Peter became. The memory of the awful things he saw might not perhaps have been able to make him keen enough. But Peter had one memory more — the denial; and this too reminded him of that same sight. He could not, I suppose, in any case forget what he had seen and experienced. It was impossible that his witness about that could be silenced. But that glance of love which overtook Peter on his way to perdition reminded him day and night of what *he* himself had to " overtake." [1] [VIII. A. 129, 130.]

Christ loved the man he saw — the man who had become so different from his former self that he denied Christ. [VIII. 3. 36(11).] We too have a duty to love the people we see; the duty of finding, in the workaday world of actuality, those we are to love in a special way; and to love these is to love those we see. [VIII. B. 36(5).] This is a love that does not spend much time or effort in finding its object, but is far more concentrated on discovering that the chosen one is lovable, and on being able to go on loving him, however different he has become. [VIII. B. 36(9).]

If Christ had merely been a man, then manifestly Peter would not have denied him. Peter was too deep and honest to betray a fellow man. Had he simply regarded Christ as a man, then I imagine he could have endured the thought of this man's being treated as he was. He would not have forgotten himself as he did, but would have remained faithful to his friend. But the seeming madness that Christ, being God, had everything in his power, and could at any moment have called legions of angels to his aid — it was this that utterly overwhelmed Peter. [VIII. A. 370; J 706.]

PRAYER

O my God, even when I went wrong, thy governance was with me; it was thy governance that allowed this to happen, and immediately embodied it lovingly in thy fatherly purpose for me, lovingly overruling innumerable possibilities, so that even this error became beneficial to me. [X³. A. 222.]

[1] The word " overtake " is unexpected but full of forceful meaning. Peter had been " caught " by Christ's love in the very act of denial; he must " catch " others by his witness.

THE TRAITOR — I

Then entered Satan into Judas surnamed Iscariot, being of the number of the twelve. And he went his way, and communed with the chief priests and captains, how he might betray him unto them. (Luke 22:3, 4.)

Christ says, " I myself have chosen them [the twelve] and yet one of them shall betray me." (John 6:10.) These words may be variously understood, but it is almost as if there were here a hint of the voluntary nature of Christ's suffering, that he himself has chosen one for an apostle who should betray him. [IX. A. 410.]

We get a very good impression of the Christianity of every age by seeing the way it regards Judas.

Abraham a Sancta Clara [1] is naïvely convinced that Judas was the basest of all scoundrels, about whom we only have to say every conceivable ill, but not try to explain him. Daub [2] becomes far too deeply metaphysical about it. [IX. A. 470.]

It is not unthinkable that Christ in his earlier conversations — just to show his disciples that his Kingdom was not of this world, and just to show them how very easy it could be to mistake its identity — may have pointed out to them how, by a single stroke, he could make the whole thing into an earthly kingdom and himself into an earthly Messiah. Then he may have taken the opportunity to warn them about the way in which they preached his doctrine; because the really decisive thing lies forever in " the second instance," [3] i.e., the *manner* in which the truth is spoken,

[1] An Augustinian monk living in Vienna in the seventeenth century.
[2] A contemporary German Protestant theologian and metaphysician, whose *Zeitschrift* and other works Kierkegaard used to read.
[3] By this Kierkegaard means the way in which the gospel is not only preached at first hand, but how secondly it reflects or reduplicates itself in the preacher.

in the "reduplication" [1] of the truth in existence and deed. A man can, e.g., preach that a kingdom is not of this world, without seeing that the whole thing has become worldliness by the manner he preaches it.

Yet, as I said, Christ had perhaps pointed out to his disciples, in earlier conversations, how near the one kingdom lies to the other, and that only a little push is needed to make the whole thing worldly. And perhaps this is what moved Judas to betray him. He may have wanted to force him to give the thing a different turn by that little push.

Or, another explanation, Judas may perhaps have been a skeptic, who, in his mistrust, could not quite believe in the holiness of Christ, but had a worldly-wise suspicion that there must be some ambition lurking in Christ. So he ventures on an experiment, to bring out the suspected ambition. He did not in the least imagine that the catastrophe would be so terrible. Hence his words, "I have betrayed innocent blood." There is something in these words that suggests that now for the first time he is entirely convinced that Christ was the Pure One. How was this? Because now Christ had stood the test, and remained true to himself.

On the whole, then, Judas must be regarded as much more than a mere scoundrel. Christ's words, "I have chosen them," applied to Judas as much as to the rest. And the whole position ought to be treated far more factually than does the point of view of Sancta Clara, which merely condemns without trying to understand. [IX. A. 474.]

PRAYER

Father in heaven, when the thought of thee wakens in our soul, let it not waken as an agitated bird which flutters confusedly about, but as a child waking from sleep with a celestial smile. [II. A. 320; J 248.]

_____

[1] I.e., the way in which it is shown forth in life.

THE TRAITOR — II

Then one of the twelve, called Judas Iscariot, went unto the chief priests, and said unto them, What will ye give me, and I will deliver him unto you? And they covenanted with him for thirty pieces of silver. And from that time he sought opportunity to betray him. (Matt. 26:14–16.)

He was a thief, and had the bag, and bare what was put therein. (John 12:6.)

The Lord Jesus, the same night in which he was betrayed, took bread. (I Cor. 11:23.)

Judas shows that until the last he was a judge of money, by getting thirty pieces of silver for one so despised as Christ was at that time. Or else he just found the chief priests at an opportune moment. [X¹. A. 164.]

There are those who have almost wanted to upbraid Christ for putting a man like Judas in charge of the bag. Was it not " irresponsible " of him, seeing Judas had a tendency to pilfering? But we should the rather say, What faith and love on Christ's part! For the boldest but yet the best means of saving such a man, is to show unconditional confidence in him. If that does not help him, then as a rule it means he cannot be helped. [X¹. A. 364.]

It was in the night in which he was betrayed [that Jesus instituted the Sacrament of Love]. Or rather he was already betrayed. Judas was already bought to sell him; the betrayer was but " seeking opportunity " to betray him to the chief priests " without a tumult." To do this he chose the stillness of the night in which Christ, for the last time, was assembled with his disciples. [X. p. 296; CD p. 257.]

If I may speak for a moment quite humanly, I would say that Christ at least had this advantage, that Judas quite simply, and as everybody knew, was the traitor; and therefore Christ has the chance of showing his superiority toward him. But as the world becomes shrewder and shrewder, it also becomes baser and baser, and its baseness more and more cunning. In modern style, the traitor would be so shrewd that ultimately Christ himself would be the only one who saw that he was the traitor, while the others, even the apostles, would just think that Judas was his true friend. By this the Exalted One himself is brought into the difficulty that he must inform against Judas — and perhaps not be even understood or believed. And thereby the impression likewise of the exalted one himself is weakened. [XI[1]. A. 132.]

PRAYER

Lord Jesus Christ, there is so much that will keep us back and draw us to itself. Everyone has something, and all of us much. But thou art eternally the most strong. Draw us then the more strongly to thee. We call thee our Deliverer, because thou didst come to the world to deliver us from all the bonds, the unworthy worries, which we put upon ourselves, and to break the heavy chain of our sins. We call thee Saviour, that so thou mayest save us, and deliver us from all these things. For this was God's will, which thou didst fulfill and make possible, even our sanctification. To this end thou didst descend to earth's lowly meadows; and for this didst thou ascend up on high, in order to draw us unto thee. [VIII. A. 372.]

CHRIST AND BARABBAS — A CONTRAST

Therefore when they were gathered together, Pilate said unto them, Whom will ye that I release unto you? Barabbas, or Jesus which is called Christ? (Matt. 27:17.)

Christ was mocked, spat upon, crucified — so deep was his degradation. And yet there is one little feature that perhaps most strongly and appallingly betokens his degradation. Possibly you do not know this; you have never heard it mentioned. Or you have heard it so often that you do not feel it. Look then. There was a notorious highwayman, Barabbas. It was *he* whom the people demanded to be released. Is it not true that contrasts throw light upon each other? Christ stands contrasted with Barabbas; yes, and the cry, " Crucify " stands contrasted with " Let Barabbas live." [VIII. A. 477.]

Of all appalling contrasts, the cry " Live Barabbas " is the worst. It reveals how utterly removed Christ was from getting justice in this world! Spiritual analogies are not lacking. It is customary to point out the implications of the words, " Crucify him." I should like to stress the implications of the words, " Let Barabbas live." [VIII. A. 471.]

There have been multitudes of people who have stood in about the same relationship to Jesus as Barabbas did, who was called " Jesus Barabbas." [1] The word " Barabbas " is about the same as the Danish N.N. It merely means *filius patris*, " son of his father."
(It is a pity we know nothing more about Barabbas. It seems to me that in many ways he could be a kind of parallel to the Wandering Jew. The rest of his life must have been strangely spent. Did he, one wonders, become a Christian? It would be and make a good subject for a poem to let him appear and bear witness for Christ, filled with His divine power.) [II. A. 346; J 258.]

It was not because the crowd were so fond of Barabbas, but because they so passionately hated Christ, that they expressed themselves thus.[2] [VIII. C. 3(19).]

[1] In a few cursive mss.; in the Armenian Version; and in some copies of the Jerusalem Syriac, the word " Jesus " comes before " Barabbas " in Matt. 27:16, 17. Pilate's question then runs: " Whom will ye that I release unto you? Jesus Barabbas, or Jesus which is called Christ? "
[2] This is a note in Kierkegaard's Bible.

PRAYER

If I had the choice between being the greatest of men without thee, and but a hair of the head which is numbered by thee, I would choose the latter. I am not indeed more than the least before thee, and I wish not to be more than any other man. Even though I am thus only little before thee, this little — this being nothing before thee — is for me infinitely much. All else is to me worth nothing — absolutely nothing. [VI. C. 161.]

THE SLEEPING DISCIPLES

And he cometh unto the disciples, and findeth them asleep, and saith unto Peter, What, could ye not watch with me one hour?
Watch and pray, that ye enter not into temptation: the spirit indeed is willing, but the flesh is weak. (Matt. 26:40, 41.)

What infinite sorrow there is in finding the disciples asleep three times! And then at last to say, " Sleep on now, it is over." [1] Alas! To fight alone — the only sympathy being that the others are asleep; looking so indifferent, as though it were no concern of theirs. [VIII. A. 582.]

This is how human nature always stands in relation to the divine: the disciples sleep — while Christ suffers. It is this urge to sleep which, according to how great it is, reveals whether we have any spirituality or not. I do not suggest that the disciples were indolent, or that they were so indifferent. No, they slept from suf-

[1] The English version of course says, " Sleep on now and take your rest " (Matt. 26:45 and Mark 14:41). The modern Danish version says, " Do you still sleep and take rest? " The version K. had, says, " It is over."

fering (for a man can become so weary through suffering that he falls asleep).

But the more spirituality, the more alertness. And therefore it is an infinite and absolute suffering for One who is God, to become a particular human being. For Spirit is utter wakefulness and activity; humanity is more or less sleepiness. [IX. A. 367.]

Jesus is sorrowful because they could not watch with him one hour; that is, watch for his sake. But at the same time he forgets himself, and gives them what is tantamount to an exhortation to watch for themselves, not him: "Watch and pray that ye enter not into temptation. The spirit indeed is willing but the flesh is weak." (v. 41.)

Verse 45, "Sleep on now and take your rest. All is over, the Son of man is betrayed . . ." shows that the exhortation to watch and pray was for their sake not his, whose fate was now sealed and his course clear.[1] [VIII. C. 3(18).]

Simon Peter, "could you not watch with me one hour?" Here Christ is for a moment a suffering mortal, who, for his own sake, wants sympathy from another person. But at the same moment he is also their Teacher. He says, "Watch and pray that ye enter not into temptation." That is, "Watch and pray not for my sake but for your own." [X⁴. A. 163.]

PRAYER

Thou my God and Father! The question of my salvation concerns no other being but me — and thee. Should there then not remain uncertainty in fear and trembling until the last, I being what I am, and thou what thou art, I on earth, thou in heaven — a difference infinitely great — I a sinner, thou the Holy One? Should there not, ought there not, must there not, be fear and trembling till the last? Was it not the fault of the foolish virgins

---

[1] Slightly expanded. This is a note written by K. in his New Testament. For "verse 45" K. first wrote "verse 43" and then crossed it out with ink and wrote "44." But I think he must mean 45.

that they became sure, and went to sleep; while the wise virgins kept awake? But what is it to keep awake? It is uncertainty in fear and trembling. And what is faith but an empty fantasy, if it be not awake? And when faith is not awake, what is it but that same pernicious feeling of security which ruined the foolish virgins? [X. p. 247; CD p. 219.]

CHRIST BEFORE PILATE

And when he was accused of the chief priests and elders, he answered nothing. (Matt. 27:12.)

Every one that is of the truth heareth my voice. Pilate saith unto him, What is truth? (John 18:37, 38.)

Pilate therefore went forth again, and saith unto them, Behold, I bring him forth to you, that ye may know that I find no fault in him. Then came Jesus forth, wearing the crown of thorns, and the purple robe. And Pilate saith unto them, Behold the man! (John 19:4, 5.)

Christ kept silence. There are two reasons for keeping quite silent. Either because one hasn't a word to say in one's defense, or because it would be an outrageous untruth to say a single word in one's defense. [X[1]. A. 285; J 960.]

Pilate's words, " What is truth? " really say the same thing as when he said, " See what a Man! " [1] For Christ who is the Truth, stands before Pilate; and therefore " What is truth? " means [though Pilate could not have known it] " Here, in Christ standing before me, I can see what truth is, revealed on earth." [X[1]. A. 159.]

[1] So the Danish version which Kierkegaard quotes. The English version says, " Behold the man."

In religion, the greatest weakness [as it appears in Christ] is the greatest power. Therefore Christ has no scepter in his hand, but only a reed, the sign of weakness. And yet at that very moment he has the greatest power. To command the whole world with a scepter does not show nearly so much power as being able to command it with only a reed, i.e., command it in his weakness, which is the divine way. A ruler in purple is not nearly so great as a ruler in rags. A ruler who really feels his power, even if he actually can wear the purple, may sometimes be seen preferring to command in an old coat, or some such garment. This, however, is a very poor analogy to the divine. The divine position is that "greatest weakness *is* greatest power." The analogy only plays at laying aside the insignia, whereas in terms of the divine, this must be done seriously. In utter earnestness, and physically understood, one must be in the position of the completest weakness. [X^4. A. 209.]

The words, "See what a Man," are really the judgment of the human race upon itself, showing how prostituted it was.

The God-man had never lost patience, or turned the tables, by saying, "I am not in the least akin to you." No, he continually revealed how entirely he *was* akin to them.

But the race could not control itself as he did. It said: "We have no affinity with you. Look what sort of person you are" [i.e., how degraded you are compared with us].

The God-man wants to show what it is to be a man. He wishes to elevate humanity to affinity with God. The race thinks it knows better and says, "We have no affinity with you."

This is the prostitution of the human race. At that moment, the race had sunk below the human level, and had really become an animal. [XI^1. A. 236.]

PRAYER

Lord Jesus, who didst suffer when Pilate said, "Behold the man," it is not the wild agitation, not the blind raging mob that scornfully cries thus. No, it is one clad in purple, a person of distinction, who speaks thus out of compassion. He would make thee into a helpless creature, a pitiful object for the compassion of the multitude. But thou didst learn obedience from the things thou didst suffer. Only he who really can keep silence can really act, for silence is of the heart. [VIII. p. 397 and p. 105; GS p. 53 and PA p. 49.]

HOW CHRIST'S PASSION DISTURBS

And so Pilate, willing to content the people, released Barabbas unto them, and delivered Jesus, when he had scourged him, to be crucified. (Mark 15:15.)

Of the Passion narrative it can be said that it is the most moving event (as regards Christ) and the most disturbing event (from the point of view of the bystanders) that ever happened or could be conceived. For it is always true of the life of Christ, that here *is* ideality. It is not here the case, as it usually is with historical narratives, that because they are not as a rule purely ideal, therefore the poet can add ideality to his narrative. Here the ideal is the historic; which is the greatest contradiction possible. And moreover it indicates how Christianity, in its pure ideality, bursts asunder the whole of existence, as it burst the grave and the veil of the temple. [X⁴. A. 208.]

The thing that people were most of all afraid of was that Christ might be dangerous to Caesar: yet Pilate was no longer afraid when Christ was scourged.

And then Christ became dangerous not only to Caesar but to the Gods of Caesar. [X⁴. A. 209.]

PRAYER

O Lord Jesus Christ, thou art the most strong. We call thee our Saviour and Redeemer, since thou didst come to earth to loose us from the fetters wherewith we are bound, or wherewith we have bound ourselves, and to save the lost. This was thy work; and thou hast completed it and shalt complete it till the end of the world. [XII. p. 173; TC p. 151.]

THE PENITENT THIEF

And one of the malefactors which were hanged railed on him, saying, If thou be Christ, save thyself and us. But the other answering rebuked him, saying, Dost not thou fear God, seeing thou art in the same condemnation? And we indeed justly; for we receive the due reward of our deeds: but this man hath done nothing amiss. And he said unto Jesus, Lord, remember me when thou comest into thy kingdom. And Jesus said unto him, Verily I say unto thee, To-day shalt thou be with me in paradise. (Luke 23:39–43.)

"Verily, verily"

O how divine a thing to say upon the cross what Christ says to the thief! All, all, all, even God in heaven by whom he is "forsaken," witness against him. But he, entirely unchanged, still with the same trustworthiness as ever, says from the cross, "Verily I say unto thee, Today shalt thou be with me in Paradise." [X⁵. A. 131.]

There is a very beautiful thought in Tersteegen's sermon [1] about the thief on the cross. He says that Christ's prayer, "Father

[1] K. possessed a volume of this German author's works, published in Essen, 1841. The sermon is on pages 145 ff. K. is writing in 1849.

forgive them for they know not what they do," became a kind of
sermon or word which converted the thief, who was deeply affected by Christ's love in praying for his enemies. And Tersteegen in the same sermon makes good use of the fact that the thief's
faith was immediately put to the test. For very soon afterward
He who had promised him that he should be with Him in paradise sighs and says, " My God, my God, why hast thou forsaken
me? " And this was he upon whom the thief had built his hope!
[X¹. A. 484.]

OUR CONSCIOUSNESS OF SIN BINDS US TO CHRIST
(BECAUSE SINNERS NEED HIM)

Everyone forsook Christ; Peter the apostle denied him. Only
the thief on the cross remained faithful to him to the end, and at
the last moment. But the consciousness of his sin bound him to
Christ — and also the fact that he was at the point of death.

But what faith! To believe that he who is in " the same condemnation," despised, mocked, spat upon, cursed, nailed to a
cross — to believe that his word meant something; to think that
he is God, who gives one a place in paradise; and to keep this
faith when this is added, that the Crucified himself cried, " My
God, my God, why hast thou forsaken me? "

Oh, there is so much preaching to the effect that Christianity is
the direct communication of God to men. But really — that a person despised and cursed by all, condemned as a criminal, nailed
to a cross — when he says, " Believe in me that I am God " —
Good heavens! is this direct communication? [X³. A. 180, 181.]

PRAYER

Deep in my soul thou didst put the blessed assurance that thou
art love. Then thou didst treat me as a father treats a child, im-
pressing the same thing upon me yet once more, proving to me
over and over again that thou art love. Then thou wert silent for
a time. Thou wouldest that I should now make trial of myself
without any proofs from thee, to see whether I could be the same
when proofs were lacking. That confused everything for me. I

became anxious and afraid; so much so that I felt this was infinitely too high for me. I was afraid I had gone too far, had been too forward, had suffered thee too long; and that therefore it was a punishment that this experience happened to me. One worry at any rate, I said, thou must exempt me from: the worry of thinking this was my fault. Ungrateful wretch that I was! As though it was my previous goodness that caused thee hitherto to show me thy love. One worry, I said, thou must spare me from, namely that it was my many failings that have made thee tired of me. Ungrateful wretch that I was! As though it was because of my wisdom and deserts that thou hadst loved me before. O wicked vain heart, which really wants to make capital out of the past; not only having perceived the blessedness of the fact that God is love, and that he reveals this to us, but lyingly thinking that we nevertheless, though but a little, could ever have been worthy of that love, even if only in compassion with our present unworthiness.

Oh, no, no! God be praised that it was never because of my worthiness that God has loved me. This very fact gives me good cheer. For otherwise a man might any moment die of fear lest the next moment he may be no longer worthy. [X³. A. 227.]

" MY GOD, MY GOD "

Now from the sixth hour there was darkness over all the land unto the ninth hour. And about the ninth hour Jesus cried with a loud voice, saying, Eli, Eli, lama sabachthani? that is to say, My God, my God, why hast thou forsaken me? (Matt. 27:45, 46.)

This humiliation is the last extreme of suffering. Among those who have been followers in the strictest sense, namely, the blood witnesses, you will find faint intimations of this same experience (i.e., of feeling forsaken by God). Yet . . . he had said that he was the only begotten Son of the Father, one with the Father. But if they two are one, how can the Father at any moment forsake him? And yet he says, " My God, my God, why hast thou forsaken me? " So it was not true after all that he was one with the Father! O extremest limit of more than human suffering! A human heart would have broken a little earlier. The God-man alone has to see this last suffering right through. And then he dies. [XII. p. 402; FSE p. 85.]

The words, " My God, my God, why hast thou forsaken me," have been understood as a nemesis, that he who had had so much in his power had not been prudent enough to make sure of his own future — and so on. It is (if I may speak in purely human fashion about this) as if Christ as a human being had become so lost in his relationship to God that all else had gone into oblivion for him. The words suggest that the consummation is now very close at hand. He is feeling, for the last time, the yawning abyss of separation between being man and being with God. And this in turn is the last token of what is to come next, namely, being in bliss with God. [IX. A. 103.]

Human categories, when applied to Christ, have a disturbing way of being the wrong way round. If, for example, we could speak quite humanly about Christ, then we must certainly say that the words, " My God, my God, why hast thou forsaken me," express impatience and falsity. Only when God says the words can they be true; and therefore they are equally true when the God-man says them. And because they are true, they express the greatest possible pain. [X¹. A. 245; J 902.]

When Christ cried, " My God, my God, why hast thou forsaken me? " it was terrible for Christ, and that is the usual explanation. But it seems to me that it must have been still more terrible for God to hear. To be unchangeable (as God is) — how terrible! Yet no. It is not this that is the terrible thing, but to be thus unchangeable and also to be love! O infinite depths of unfathomable sorrow!

Alas, how much have I, a poor human being, suffered in this respect; this contradiction in not being able to be changed, and yet to love! Alas, how much I have suffered! And this helps me, though only from far away, far away, to form to myself a weak picture of the suffering of divine love. [XI¹. A. 422; J 1345.]

MEDITATION AND PRAYER

With confidence and faith in God, I would rather receive from his hand whatever he may send than have pleasant conditions when I myself have prudently avoided a danger which was set before me to meet. Certainly I long for encouragement. If God shall give it me, with heartfelt thanks I receive it. But the nervousness that makes my heart stand still, the nervousness that comes over me at the thought that possibly I had let God call but prudently had gone out of the way — that I could not bear. God compels no one. He tells us beforehand of the dangers, he terrifies us by the help of fear-creating imaginations: and he looks upon us and says: " Go dauntlessly forward, my child. But if you are afraid, I will not compel you." Oh, is there any way more compelling than this?

A few words, O Lord! When I go forward like this, I am, humanly speaking, prepared for the worst. But yet, yet, I cannot do otherwise.

I do not expect a pleasant result, humanly speaking, even though I believe it possible. But one thing is certain. Thou wilt not desert me; thou wilt remain with me in a cheerful courage which is worth infinitely more than all the world's good days. [VIII. A. 560.]

CHRIST CRUCIFIED

Thou that destroyest the temple, and buildest it in three days, save thyself. (Matt. 27:40.)

They are really saying the converse of the truth. Had Christ saved himself, he would not have destroyed the temple (i.e., upset the Jewish system).

Thus we may learn something even from the mockery. [X². A. 73.]

If thou be the Son of God, come down from the cross. (Matt. 27:40.)

No. It is just because he is God's Son that he *was* upon the cross. Or, to put it otherwise, just because he was upon the cross, he proves that he is the Son of God.

But humanity cannot grasp the divine mind. Humanity's proofs and conclusions are topsy-turvy. It would conclude that he was the Son of God, if he came down from the cross. But if he did, he would just not be the Son of God. [X². A. 73.]

He saved others, himself he cannot save. (Matt. 27:42.)

And no wonder. For if he were to save himself, he could not save others. Precisely in order to save others, he will not save himself. Here again, mockery says something quite different from what it thinks it is saying.

O save not thyself, thou Saviour of the world, else were the world lost! [X². A. 73.]

That Jesus Christ died for my sins shows certainly how great his grace is, but also how great my sins are, and how infinitely far I am from God; so that God will deal with me only upon condition that Christ should die for me. We can therefore say that such a sacrifice, such a mediatorial act, was necessary, both to express God's majesty and win man's respect. Through that act I may dare to turn to him, and then he will have dealings with me. Humanity could not have invented atonement in this deepest sense, because no man could, by himself, raise his thoughts to the height of God's mind. Only God himself knows how infinitely exalted he is. And here the remarkable thing is, that precisely by his condescension, God indirectly reveals his exaltation also. " I am willing," he says, " to let myself be reconciled with man [what condescension!] on this condition, that my Son lets himself be offered for you." What infinite distance of exaltation, if that is the only condition! [X². A. 189.]

As our Pattern, Christ reveals something which of course no human being can attain to, namely, absolute closeness to God in everything. Hence the word of mockery, " He holdeth to God, let us see whether God has pleasure in him." [1] The mischief in this mockery is not something special to those Jews. It is in every man. For there is conflict between God and man, and a choice must be made as to whom we will hold to. The more we cling to God, the more we strive that our lives shall be pure and disinterested, and then our strife is devoted. [X². A. 317.]

PRAYERS

He whom thou dost call thy friend, who walks in the light of thy countenance, seeks (not without trembling) the meeting of friendship with thee, who alone art mighty. How then shall the sinner dare to seek thee, the God of righteousness? He seeks thee in confession of his sins. [V. p. 201; TCS p. 1 f.]

O the infinite reliance we may place upon thee, the good! Wherever in the world a man may be, on whatever road he fares, when he would have an undivided will, there is a road that leads him to thee. [VIII. p. 154; PH p. 41.]

[1] Matt. 27:43. In English, " He trusted in God; let him deliver him now, if he will have him."

THE RISEN CHRIST

*And, behold, two of them went that same day to a village
called Emmaus, which was from Jerusalem about threescore fur-
longs. And they talked together of all these things which had
happened. And it came to pass, that, while they communed together and reasoned, Jesus himself drew near, and went with
them. But their eyes were holden that they should not know
him. . . . And beginning at Moses and all the prophets, he ex-
pounded unto them in all the Scriptures the things concerning
himself. And they drew nigh unto the village, whither they
went: and he made as though he would have gone further. But
they constrained him, saying, Abide with us; for it is toward
evening, and the day is far spent. And he went in to tarry with
them. . . . And their eyes were opened, and they knew him;
and he vanished out of their sight. (Luke 24:13–16, 27–29, 31.)*

The Saviour walks unseen on the way with these two sad people. In fact he always does walk with us, but though the highest
is exceedingly close, our eyes are holden.

Eternity, and all that is highest, accompanies us through all the
different ages of our life. But we are not fully observant of it. We
do not look closely enough. We wish, sigh, and are occupied. Yet
just as we can tell the time by observing the shadows our bodies
cast, so we can tell a person's maturity by how near he thinks the
highest is to him. Youth and manhood go by, and only when eventide comes and the day is far spent does a man fully understand
that the highest lies exceedingly close, and has walked by his side
all his life — and perhaps he has not appreciated it. God grant
that then it may remain with him! [VIII. A. 56.]

"He made as though he would have *gone farther*. But they
constrained him saying, Abide with us for it is toward evening."

This is as it were a picture indicating the relationship between
Christ, the Pattern, and the believer. The Pattern is so far in ad-

vance that even with a single step the believer is disheartened.
Yet the believer must still strive, and the Pattern patiently yield
a little. Then, in spite of the believer's infinite imperfection, a
little progress is made. But it may often happen that it seems as if
the Pattern would go farther, and so much farther that his follower is lost. So the follower prays for himself saying, "Abide
with me." This abiding is what man sorely needs. But it involves
patient suffering for Christ our Pattern. [X². A. 347.]

The words "He vanished" can be understood as implying that
his vanishing was the result of their recognizing him. He cannot
be known directly. It is faith that sees. Our imaginations are given
no view of him, for such a view would correspond to the way
the gods are depicted in paganism. [X¹. A. 575.]

PRAYER
Lord Jesus Christ! All thy life didst thou endure suffering in order to save me; and alas! the time of thy suffering is not over. But
it is true, is it not? that thou wilt continue to endure suffering in
thy task of saving and redeeming — this patient suffering in having dealings with me, I who so often went astray from the right
way, or, even if I remained on the straight path, nevertheless so
often stumbled along the right way, or went creeping forward so
slowly on the right way. Infinite patience! infinite suffering of patience! How many times have I been impatient, wished to forsake thee, wished to give up everything, to take the terribly easy
way out, the way of despair: but thou didst not lose patience.
Alas, the words of thy servant that he "filled up that which was
lacking in thy sufferings" (Col. 12:14) do not apply to me. No,
I can only claim that I have increased thy sufferings, added new
ones to those thou didst once suffer in order to save me. [X². A.
343; J 1030.]

"I GO TO THE FATHER"

"Verily, verily, I say unto you, that ye shall weep and lament, but the world shall rejoice; and ye shall be sorrowful, but your sorrow shall be turned into joy." (John 16:20.)

This expresses the relationship between Christianity and the world. In the first heat, the world conquers as it seems (it rejoices — ye weep and lament). But in the second heat — ah, but really it is only Christianity that can speak of a second heat. The world is too empty and vain for there to be more than one go for it, which is no go, nothing. Christianity is really the second time (as " spirit " is the second time),[1] and then shall sorrow be turned to joy. [IX. A. 20.]

A little while, and ye behold me no more: and again a little while, and ye shall see me.[2] (John 16:16.)

With regard to temptation it is also true that it is only for " a little while." Temptation has its power " at the moment." Fearful are the powers it has to alarm us, and as it were compress everything into a moment — and in the next moment it is powerless. [X². A. 161.]

PRAYER

Father in heaven! From thy hand we would receive everything. Thou stretchest out that mighty hand of thine, and seizest the wise in their folly; thou stretchest out that mighty hand of thine, and the worlds perish. Thou openest that gentle hand of thine, and satisfiest all that lives with blessing. And if sometimes it seemeth thee good to withdraw thine hand from us, oh, still we know

[1] Kierkegaard is thinking of being born again of the Spirit.
[2] John 16:16 ff. was in Kierkegaard's day, and still is, the Gospel for the third Sunday after Easter.

of a surety that thou shuttest it only to open it again, and fill all that lives with blessing.[1] [II. A. 554.]

"IT IS EXPEDIENT FOR YOU THAT I GO AWAY"

Nevertheless I tell you the truth; It is expedient for you that I go away: for if I go not away, the Comforter will not come unto you; but if I depart, I will send him unto you. (John 16:7.)

In a certain sense we may, even humanly speaking, put a thing in quite the opposite way from what we otherwise should. It is customary, for example, to say it was natural that the disciples should feel forsaken when Christ went away; that a miracle would be needed to strengthen them; that of course they must have felt stronger as long as Christ was with them — and so on. We forget what simple human experience teaches. A disciple leads a kind of stunted existence so long as his master lives with him. The disciple cannot, so to say, become himself. He wavers between being always nervous about his teacher's censure (which is so near at hand) and always wanting to lean on his teacher. The law of maturity is always this: in order to achieve his full strength, a man must not have visible help, but only invisible. The same divine help which, as being invisible, is so absolutely helpful is, in a human manner of speaking, a cause of difficulty when it is visible. That is undoubtedly the meaning of Christ's words, that it is expedient that he go away, else the Spirit cannot come.[2] [X[1]. A. 624; J 950.]

The most copious prophecy that has ever been uttered, was

[1] Cf. *Edifying Discourses* I. 34 (III. 45).
[2] John 16:5 ff. was in Kierkegaard's day, and still is, the Gospel for the fourth Sunday after Easter.

when Christ said, " It is good for you that I go away." Then was
the time when Christ's earthly existence had reached such a degree of maturity that his body was " dry," so to say, as fruit is dry
when its time is over; when the whole fullness of his Godhead
could no longer be contained in earthly form as an *individual* existence. [II. A. 369.]

PRAYER

Lord Jesus Christ, the inestimable treasure of thy disciples,
their daily bread of gladness [V. p. 187; ED IV. p. 137], their expectation of bliss, how was it possible for them to understand
thy words, " It is expedient for you that I go away? " Only by
faith! For then the Comforter comes, whom thou wilt send. He is
indeed the dispenser of grace — the grace that thou didst win for
us. He is indeed our Comforter in this respect also, that thou,
Lord Jesus, as our perfect Pattern, dost put a demand which no
man can fulfill. So long therefore as thou wast present on earth,
thou wast the inevitable doom of man. But thou our perfect Pattern didst die, and thy death was an atonement. Now thou art so
transformed as to be forever grace. Be thou then gracious to us
thy servants, even with respect to our imperfect efforts to resem-
ble thee, thou perfect Pattern. [From X². A. 451 ad.]

THE ASCENSION

And whither I go ye know, and the way ye know. Thomas
saith unto him, Lord, we know not whither thou goest; and how
can we know the way? Jesus saith unto him, I am the way, the
truth, and the life: no man cometh unto the Father, but by me.
(John 14:4–6.)

Christ is the way. It is his own word, so certainly it must be the
truth.

(*a*) And this way is *narrow*. Look upon him, and you see immediately that the way is narrow.

(*b*) And this way which is Christ, this narrow way, *is narrow at the very beginning*. He was born in poverty and wretchedness, plotted against by the mighty while still a child, so that his poor parents had to flee with him. Thereafter he lives in poverty and lowliness, and has not where to lay his head. He is tempted every instant of his life — that is to say, he has it all the time in his power to take his calling, his task, in vain [but he would not yield to such a temptation].

(*c*) *And this way which is Christ, this narrow way, becomes narrower and narrower as it goes on, until the very last, until death.*

(*d*) And *Christ is the way*. He goes up into a mountain, and a cloud receives him out of their sight. He ascends into heaven — and he is the way!

On Ascension Day it ought to be remembered that the way is narrow. Otherwise we might easily take the ascension in vain. Remember! his way was narrow until the last. Death had to intervene before the ascension could follow. It was not in the middle of the way that he went into heaven, not even at the end of the way, for the way ended in the cross and grave. The ascension does not lie in straightforward continuation with what went before. No indeed! A narrow way in this life, even when it leads to victory, never leads so high that it becomes an ascension into heaven. *He* ascends into heaven. No one else ever conquered thus! A cloud received him out of their sight. No one was ever lifted thus in triumph from the earth! They saw him no more. No one else had such a triumph as their last experience.

He sits at the right hand of power. Then his triumph did not end with his ascension? No. With ascension his triumph begins. Never has other man triumphed thus!

He is to come again with his hosts of angels. Then his triumph did not end when he took his place at the right hand of power? No. That was but the beginning of the end.

O eternal Conqueror!

In which way are you walking? Remember (and I am saying this also to myself) that not every narrow way is the way of Christ, nor do all lead to heaven. There are human sufferings enough, only too many; sickness and poverty and misunderstanding — who can name them all? And the way of these is narrow. But that which distinguishes the Christian narrow way from the ordinary human narrow way is the element of free will. Christ *chose* humiliation. This, in the strictest sense, is the narrow way. If you also go along this way as a Christian, it leads to heaven where he entered, he the ascended Christ.

People have doubted about the ascension. Yes, but who? Any of those whose life bore the mark of an imitator? Any of those who left all to follow Christ? No. Those whose lives were marked by " imitation " have had no doubt about the ascension; first, because their lives were too strenuous to be able to sit in idleness and deal with reasons and doubts. (They are rather like a warrior who owns a gorgeous robe. He knows well that he has it, but he never looks at it because his whole life is passed in daily combat and peril.) Moreover, they pressingly need another sort of comfort than that which earth affords. They need the ascension of their Lord and Master, and believingly they press through to the ascension. Where there is need, there the need itself produces that which it needs.

And now you, dear reader, how is it with you? Do you doubt the ascension? If so, say to yourself: " I know very well from whence doubt comes, namely, that I have been lenient with myself in this matter of ' imitation.' My life has not been strenuous enough. I have spared myself the danger of witnessing for truth and against falsehood." All doubt is really self-denunciation. Make then to yourself and God this confession, and one of two things will happen. Either you will be moved to venture farther out in the direction of " imitation " — and then certainty about the ascension comes at once — or you will humble yourself for having spared yourself. You will say humbly, " If God will be so gracious as to treat me as a child who is almost entirely spared from the sufferings of 'imitation,' I will at least not be a naughty child who doubts the ascension as well." And if for a good cause you live forsaken, persecuted, ridiculed, you will find that you do not doubt the ascension, because you need it. [XII. pp. 394 ff.; FSE pp. 75 ff.]

I go to prepare a place for you. (*John 14:2.*)

In teaching a child to walk, we mysteriously get ahead of the child, and then turn toward the child to receive it. That is to say, we do not walk by the child's side, but are ourselves (oh, how delicious if we are the mother!) the goal to which the child shall walk by itself. So Christ mysteriously "went before" us at the ascension. He does not go by his disciples' side, but is himself the goal, and turns himself toward the believer. He stretches out his arms just as a mother does, if perchance she stands so far away that she cannot get near the child, then she stretches out her arms and moves them as if she were all the time grasping the child, although there is too great a distance between them for this. So solicitous is the mother — more solicitous she could not be, because otherwise the child would not learn to walk. [V.B. 237.]

PRAYER

Lord Jesus Christ, thou who knewest thy fate in advance, and yet didst not draw back; thou who didst suffer thyself to be born in poverty and lowliness, and thereupon in poverty and lowliness didst bear the sin of the world in suffering until, hated, forsaken, mocked, spat upon, and at last forsaken of God, thou didst bow thy head in a death of shame: oh, thou didst lift up thy head again, thou everlasting conqueror, thou who wast not victorious over thine enemies in life, but in death wast victorious over death; thou didst lift up thine head, forever victorious, thou who art ascended into heaven! Would that we might follow after thee! [XII. pp. 394 ff.; FSE pp. 75 ff.]

ON SPEAKING WITH TONGUES — SOBERLY

And they were all amazed and marveled, saying one to an-other, Behold, are not all these which speak Galileans?

And how hear we every man in our own tongue, wherein we were born?

Others mocking said, These men are full of new wine. (Acts 2:7, 8, 13.)

It is true not only of the speech on that first Whitsunday that it is a speaking with tongues, but that all the language which is used in the New Testament is a speaking with tongues, even though it be written in the same words, and the same language, that we all use. To be persecuted from city to city, flayed alive, and so on, and yet to say, This is sheer joy; to thank God for the grace of being scourged at the whipping post and so on — *this* is to speak with tongues. [X⁵. A. 66.]

When the apostles appeared at Pentecost, filled for the first time with the Holy Ghost, " then the people were amazed and doubted saying, What can this be? Others mocking said, they are filled with new wine." No one except the mockers offered any ex-planation, and they said that the apostles were drunk — and so early in the day, nine o'clock in the morning!

But this explanation will not do. For the surprising thing is that they were in the same condition not only that morning; no, if they were drunk, they were the same the next morning also, and the next evening, and a month later, and twenty years after, and still at the very hour of death they were drunk with that new wine, which, according to the explanation of the mockers, they had drunk that morning. O profound mockery of the mockers' expla-nation!

Here, as usual, it is clear that the world and Christianity have the most opposite conceptions. The world says of the apostles, of the apostle Peter the spokesman, " He is drunk." And the apostle Peter gives the warning, " Be sober." (I Peter 1:13.) That is to say, the worldly mind regards Christianity as drunkenness. " Only be sensible, come to yourself, see that you are sober " — so cries the worldly mind to the Christian. And the Christian says to the worldly mind, " Only be sensible, come to yourself, be sober! " It is precisely that drunken man the apostle who finds it necessary to press upon a " sober " world (sic) the warning, " Be sober." [XII. p. 435 f.; JY p. 113 f.]

PRAYER

Father in heaven! Thou art Spirit, and they that worship thee must worship thee in spirit and in truth. But how in spirit and in truth if we are not — or at any rate at least striving to be — sober? Send then thy Spirit into our hearts. He is called upon so often that he may come and bring courage and life, and power and strength. O that he first of all — for this is indeed the condition for all the rest, and the condition that all the rest may be to our good — O that he first might make us sober! [Ibid.]

THE HOLY TRINITY

No man can come to me, except the Father which hath sent me draw him: and I will raise him up at the last day. (John 6:44.)

THE GODHEAD — FATHER, SON, AND HOLY SPIRIT:
THEIR INTERRELATION

It is usual to explain the Trinity [by beginning at the human end] and saying that it is Christ who leads us to God. Man needs a Mediator in order to come to God [and that Mediator is Christ, second Person in the Trinity.]

But this is not how the New Testament, and especially John's Gospel, approaches the matter. [It begins from the divine side, showing that it is not so much a matter of man's coming to God on his own initiative as of God's drawing near to men on *His* initiative.] The proof of this lies in the fact that the very mark of our relationship to God is that we are humbled [whereas from the human standpoint we come to God to be exalted. And so indeed we are, but only if we are humbled first.]

Our relationship to God begins with the Father, or rather with our relationship to God as Father, without any Mediator. This is precisely the attitude of a little child; a simple, unaffected, naïve attitude, which treats everybody alike, recognizing no distinctions, addressing an emperor with the same familiarity as he addresses his nurse. This childlike attitude finds it quite straightforward and natural that God should be his Father.

But when a man reaches a certain point of maturity, God becomes for him so infinitely exalted that it seems presumption to call God " Father " any more, lest the word become a mere empty phrase. And God, if I may so put it, is of the same opinion.

So God refers us to the Son as Mediator. It is as if God said, " Through this Mediator I can be your Father."

Thus the Mediator appears. But this Mediator is also our Pattern. [When we realize this, we have reached a further stage; we now show a kind of] lovable youthfulness, whose mark is that in its adorable simplicity it finds no ideal too hard. It is quite natural for this youthfulness to have such an infinitely exalted Pattern; and it has the delightfully pious but illusory conviction that between these two, the Pattern and himself, there can be, in the best sense of the word, a kind of comradely equality — if only sufficient effort is made.

But when a man has reached a still further point of maturity, the Pattern in turn becomes so infinitely exalted that one does not naïvely begin striving, in this comradely sort of way, to be like the Pattern. And the Pattern too, if I may so put it, is of the same opinion. He also thinks that this would really be presumption.

Meantime there is another angle from which the Pattern may

be viewed. The Pattern is also the " Redeemer." This is the side which the aforementioned lovable youthfulness is really not aware of, because in its lovable zeal it straightway sets about trying to imitate the Pattern, finding no difficulty in the Pattern's infinite exaltation. Youthfulness, that is to say, does not discern the reason for the Pattern's infinite exaltation, namely that in him there is a qualitative difference from ordinary men. And moreover youth has an illusory conception of its own powers.

Yet the " Redemption " must not supplant the " Pattern." The Pattern is there, demanding to be striven after.

So the Pattern points away from himself to the " Spirit " (just as the Father had pointed away from himself to the Mediator), as though he would say: " You cannot naïvely start striving on your own. That would be, as doubtless you yourself feel, presumption (a thing which that lovable youthfulness was too naïve to discover; and therefore it was not guilty of any presumption in what it did). No, you must have the Spirit to help you."

Thus it comes about that it is not the Spirit who leads to the Son, and the Son who leads to the Father. No, it is the Father who points to the Son, and the Son to the Spirit. Only then does the Spirit lead to the Son and the Son to the Father.

All this, if I may dare say so, shows a certain tenacity in God about his majesty, which is nothing less than imperiousness or superiority. Nay, this is inseparable from God's being. For the more God gives himself; the more dealings he has with man; the more he draws near to man — or even by the fact that he *wills* to do so — the more is man, though elevated, brought low. For truly man is elevated by God's condescension, but only by getting an infinitely higher conception of God. And this higher conception brings him low.

How uplifting all this is! No human sovereign can secure himself against frowardness on the part of his subjects, in the way God does. But God is secure, because the nearer you come to him, the more humbled you are. That is to say, the nearer you come to him, the more infinite a conception do you get of his infinite exaltation above you, yourself the while being humbled.

"He must increase but I must decrease." (John 3:30.) That is the law for every approach to God. Though God were removed by millions of stairs he would not thereby be secured against frowardness, because such stairs might in time be climbed. But to be secured by the law of reversal that nearness is distance — what infinite majesty that is!

"But," you may say, "in a way I then lose God." How? When he increases? No, if I lose anything it is myself and my self-importance; until at last I find perfect bliss in the prayer, "He must increase but I must decrease."

This is the law for all true love. If I want to increase *at the same time* as God increases, then that certainly is self-love.

No, he must increase, and I decrease. Only he remains my Father all the same, and he becomes my Father through the Spirit in the Mediator. [X⁵. A. 23; J 1282.]

PART

II

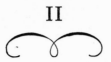

THE SERMON ON THE MOUNT

THE OTHER CHEEK

Ye have heard that it hath been said, An eye for an eye, and a tooth for a tooth: but I say unto you, That ye resist not evil: but whosoever shall smite thee on thy right cheek, turn to him the other also. (Matt. 5:38, 39.)

Augustine draws attention to the fact that this commandment was not fulfilled even by Christ himself. For when one of the high priests' servants struck him on the cheek he said, " If I have spoken evil, bear witness of the evil, but if well, why smitest thou me? " (John 18:22.) And Augustine explains it by saying, " By this conduct Christ prevented a further injustice."

Here it is the case, as I have often reflected concerning *meek*ness, that by its very facility in minimizing guilt [1] (if this be carried to extremes) it has in it this double danger: first that it almost confirms the guilty in thinking that his guilt is nothing, and secondly that the very *meek*ness can be too rigid in its leniency. For if we make a person conscious of his guilt, he may perhaps give up sinning. To a certain extent therefore, there may almost be cruelty in carrying the leniency of meekness to extremes, an almost ironic falsity.

All spiritual situations are so extraordinarily complicated, that whatever point you start from, by carrying it out too uncompromisingly, you can arrive at exactly the opposite; as in this case, meekness itself, carried out altogether inconsiderately, can to a high degree become a formidable rigidity. [X². A. 564; J 1080.]

Humanly speaking there certainly is something almost cruel about Christianity. But this cruelty is not inherent in Christianity itself; it comes about because Christianity has to exist in this sinful world, has to be revealed and developed in the sinful world. Christianity is not cruel, but the cruelty comes in through what

[1] Cf. *Gospel of Suffering*, p. 40 (VIII. p. 386).

happens to Christianity. Christianity itself is leniency and love. It is love itself, or itself is love.

Humanly speaking there certainly is something cruel in what is required of the Christian. Yet no — not in what is required of him, but in what happens to him. For what happens is not due to Christianity; it comes about partly because the Christian himself is a sinner, and partly because the world wherein he must live is sinful. Christianity only requires a man to love his fellow men with all his heart. It is not responsible for the persecutions that follow.

But can I honestly say that I wish Christianity did not demand so much, or at least not so insistently? Could I wish that it bargained, and thereby procured me a bit better days? Could I then love Christianity so deeply?

O God, it is mine own weakness which, in a weak moment makes me wish Christianity were different. But were it different, I should disapprove the very difference. [IX. A. 329.]

BLESSING ONE'S PERSECUTORS

But I say unto you, Love your enemies, bless them that curse you, do good to them that hate you, and pray for them which despitefully use you, and persecute you; that ye may be the children of your Father which is in heaven: for he maketh his sun to rise on the evil and on the good, and sendeth rain on the just and on the unjust. (Matt. 5:44, 45.)

"Bless them which persecute you." But is this possible? Think of it like this. Have you any conception how blessed it is when your converse with God increases in intimacy? Ah, but if, at the very moment when this blessedness passes all your understanding — if you then sincerely consider that the persecution of your enemies is the very thing that helped you to feel this blessedness, at such a moment is it not possible to bless them?

To bless them! That is indeed, if I may dare say so, a festal expression, indicating how indescribable is the blessedness you feel.

Just think of Socrates. When the cup of poison was offered to him, he said, " Is it permitted to make a libation? " How festive! And so the Christian, if at the moment when he feels his fellowship with God most blissfully and has to confess that he owes this for the most part to his persecutors — if then he merely says: " I will forgive them. I am not angry with them," how little festive this is! No, he must say " I bless them."

It is like the story in which a cruel stepmother casts a little girl into a well. This is discovered by the fairies, who carry the child into the happy home of Enchantment. From here the little girl sees her stepmother, and, with the most blissful token of the innocent joy of a child, kisses her hand to her, as if she were the dearest mother.

But take good care of this. Do not bother a fig about the persecutors, but take all the more care to be thus blessed in your fellowship with God. Alas, we men think most about the persecutors, and less about using the persecution so that it directs us up to God! Alas, and many even end by cursing not only their persecutors, but God also! [X². A. 513.]

ON SEEKING GOD'S KINGDOM *FIRST*

But seek ye first the kingdom of God, and his righteousness; and all these things shall be added unto you. (Matt. 6:33.)

" Pursue first the Kingdom of God." This word might be interpreted in one of two ways: either (*a*) negatively, as though a man had tried everything else and knew that he had *not* found the right thing to do, or (*b*) positively, as though a man knew that the first expression for seeking God's Kingdom first, is, in a certain sense, to do nothing; because to pursue *first* God's Kingdom is, at first, the same as to forsake all.

"Pursue God's Kingdom first." But what is it then that I must *do?* Shall I seek a job in order to do something? No, you shall first seek God's Kingdom. Shall I give all my possessions to the poor? No, you shall first seek God's Kingdom and his righteousness. Shall I go out into the world like an apostle and preach the Kingdom? No, you shall first seek God's Kingdom. But is not this in a sense to do nothing? Yes, certainly it is, in a certain sense. [IX. A. 13, 14.]

Yes certainly it is, in a certain sense nothing. You must, in the deepest sense, make yourself nothing, become nothing before God, learn to keep silent. In this silence is the beginning, which is *first* to seek God's Kingdom.

In this way (and it is a godly way), one comes to the beginning by going, in a certain sense, backward. The beginning is not that which we begin with, but arrive at. One comes at it backward. The beginning is the art of *becoming* silent. Man differs from the beasts in that he can speak, but in relation to God it may easily be his ruin that he is too willing to speak. In proportion as a man becomes more earnest in prayer, he has less and less to say, and in the end he is quite silent. He *became* silent. Indeed he became, if such a thing be possible, something still more opposed to speaking than silence is. He became a hearer. He thought that to pray was to speak. He learned that prayer is not only to keep silence, but to listen. And so it is. Prayer is not to hear oneself speak, but to arrive at silence, and continue being silent; to wait till one hears God speak.

Hence it is that the word of the Gospel, "Seek ye *first* God's Kingdom," not only says no to every question as to whether it is "this" we must do, but it says, "You shall begin by praying." Not as though prayer always begins in silence, but because when prayer really has become prayer, then it has become silence, and that is to seek first God's Kingdom. [XI. p. 19 f.; CD p. 323 f.]

The Gospel says, "Seek first God's Kingdom." Experience teaches that when men have sought their peace and joy every other way, then they turn finally, *at the very last,* to God. If a man is to succeed in getting to seek God's Kingdom first, he must begin repentantly. [X². A. 360.]

PRAYER
Father in heaven! What in society with men, and particularly when they are crowded together, we get to know with such difficulty, and what, if we have learned it elsewhere, we so easily forget in society with men, and particularly when they are crowded together, O that we may learn this now — learn silence, obedience, joy! [XI. p. 11; CD p. 315.]

ON NOT SERVING TWO MASTERS

No man can serve two masters: for either he will hate the one, and love the other; or else he will hold to the one, and despise the other. Ye cannot serve God and mammon. (*Matt.* 6:24.)

"No man can serve two masters." But look around the world amongst men, and forget not to include yourself also, and you will perhaps not find a single one of whom it is anything like true that he serves one master. It might seem that there is nothing possible but to serve two masters, since everybody does it. And yet the gospel says, "No man can serve two masters." Were there not one single person who wanted to serve one master, still the gospel would not allow itself to be impressed by the remaining millions. It does not abate anything. It repeats, "No man can serve two masters." The gospel's meaning is that to try to do so is man's un-doing.

This is how time and eternity stand toward each other: Temporally speaking, it is true that if you want to become something great in this world, to have good luck, and so on, then you must try to serve two masters. By willing one thing, you do not get far in this world; indeed, that is the very way to ruin in this world. But in eternity it is true that wanting to serve two masters is the way to perdition. [X³. A. 390.]

As for the assertion that it is not possible to serve two masters ("No man *can* serve two masters"), surely there must be a misunderstanding? For it is only too possible to do so, as the whole experience of the world attests. It would have been more understandable if the gospel had said, "No man *should* serve two masters." The other thing (serving two masters) is easy to do; and if you want to become something in this world, you must set yourself diligently to serve two or more masters. Yet perhaps the world and the gospel are speaking of two different things. The world speaks, as is natural, about this world. The gospel talks about eternity. No man can serve two masters — no, not to all eternity; and if one cannot do it in terms of the eternal, one cannot do it at all. For the fact that it seems as if one could, in these few seconds of earthly existence, is neither here nor there so far as concerns the truth as to whether one can or cannot. How a man is to fare in this world is something which the gospel (in contrast with novels, romances, lies, and other time-wasting) does not waste its time by considering. To the gospel, the seventy years of earthly existence are like an instant, and its speech hastens on to the decision of eternity. Nor does it deludingly hold out to man bright prospects for this life and for this world, when (eternally unchanged) it proclaims the eternal truth, "No man can serve two masters." [XII. p. 488; JY p. 162.]

PRAYER

O Lord Jesus Christ, it was not to plague us men but to save us, that thou didst say, " No man can serve two masters." O that we might be willing to take this word by acting after it; that is, that we may follow after thee! [XII. p. 487; JY p. 161.]

THE GLORY OF MANHOOD: A PARABLE — I

Consider the lilies of the field. (Matt. 6:28.)
Behold the fowls of the air. (Matt. 6:26.)

There was once a lily which grew in an out-of-the-way place by a little rippling brook, and lived in happy companionship with some nettles and a few other little flowers which grew nearby. The lily, to use the true description of the gospel, was more beautifully arrayed than Solomon in all his glory. Moreover she was carefree and happy all the day long. Unnoticed and blissful, the time slipped by, like the rippling brook which murmurs its song and is gone. But it happened that one day there came a little bird and visited the lily. It came again the next day. Then it stayed away for several days. Then it came again.

Now this seemed to the lily a strange and inexplicable thing: inexplicable that the bird did not remain in the same place like the little flowers nearby; strange that the bird could be so fickle. But as it so often happens, so it happened with the lily, that just because the bird was fickle, therefore she fell in love with him more and more.

This little bird was a wicked bird. Instead of putting himself in the lily's place; instead of rejoicing in her beauty and sharing the joy of her innocent bliss, the bird would make himself important by the consciousness of his freedom, and by making the lily feel her bondage. And not only so, but the little bird was also talkative. He talked fast and loose, true and false, of how in other places there were great numbers of lilies far more magnificent than she; there was also a joy and cheerfulness, a perfume, a splendor of colors, a song of the birds, which surpassed all description. So spoke the bird; and its stories ended as a rule with the remark, so humiliating for the lily, that she, in comparison with such glory, looked nothing. Indeed, she was so insignificant that it was a question whether she had any right to be called a lily at all.

So the lily began to worry; and the more she listened to the bird, the more worried she became. No longer did she sleep soundly at night. No longer did she wake up happy in the morning. She felt herself imprisoned and bound. She found the murmuring of the water wearisome, and the day long. She began to be taken up with worrying about herself and her circumstances all the day long. " It is all very well," she said to herself, " once in a while, and for the sake of a change, to listen to the murmuring of the brook. But day in and day out eternally to hear the same thing, that is much too wearisome." " It may be pleasant enough," she said to herself, " once in a while to be in an out-of-the-way place and lonely, but to be forgotten like this all my life through; to be without company, or be in company with stinging nettles, which after all are no society for a lily — that is not to be endured." " And then to look so inferior as I do," said the lily to herself, " to be so insignificant as the little bird says I am, O why was I not put in another place, and in different circumstances? O why was I not made a crown imperial? "

For that little bird had told her that the crown imperial was regarded as the most beautiful among all lilies, and was an object of envy to all other lilies. The lily noticed that unfortunately the worry was telling on her. So she talked seriously to herself; yet not so seriously that she put the worry out of her mind, but rather in such a way as to convince herself that her worry was justified. " For," she said, " my wish is no unreasonable wish. I do not ask the impossible, namely to be what I am not — a bird, for example. My wish is only to become a magnificent lily, or even perhaps the most magnificent."

During all this, the little bird flew to and fro, and her unrest was fostered by every visit and every parting. At last she confided all her heart to the bird. One evening they agreed that a change should take place next morning, which should put an end to her worries. Early next morning the little bird came. With his beak he pecked away the soil from the lily's root, so that she might be free. When this had been done, the bird took the lily under his wing and flew away. It had been arranged that the bird should fly with the lily to the place where those magnificent lilies bloomed. Then the bird was to assist in replanting her there, to see whether, by the change of place and the new surroundings, the lily might not succeed in becoming a magnificent lily, in a multifarious company, or perhaps even a crown imperial, envied by all the others.

Alas, on the way the lily withered! Had that worried lily been content with being a lily, then she would not have been worried. And had she not been worried, then she would have remained where she was; where she was in all her beauty. And had she remained there, she would have been that very lily about whom the priest spoke last Sunday when he recited the words of the Gospel, " Consider the lily . . . I say unto you that even Solomon in all his glory was not arrayed like this one."

The lily is mankind. That wicked little bird is the restless cogitation of comparison, which roams around far and wide, inconstant and fickle, acquiring an unhealthy knowledge about difference. And just as the bird did not put itself in the lily's place, so neither does comparison. By it, a person either puts himself in another's place, or another in his place. The little bird is the poet, the seducer, in a man; in other words, what is poetical and seductive in him. The poetical element is like the bird's speech, true and false, poetry and truth.[1] It is certainly true that difference exists, and there is much to be said about it. But for poetry,

[1] Cf. the title of Goethe's autobiography, *Dichtung und Wahrheit,* " Poetry and Truth."

with all its passion of despair or exultation, difference is what matters most. And that is eternally untrue.

In his concern for comparisons, the worried man at last goes so far that he forgets, by dint of difference, that he is a man; and despairingly he thinks himself to be so different from other men, that he even thinks he is different in his very manhood. That of course is what the little bird meant, when he suggested that the lily was so insignificant that it was a question whether she really was a lily at all. And the defense put up for worrying (it seems so reasonable) is always that we are not asking anything unreasonable — such as to become a bird, for example; but only to fulfill an ambition we have not yet achieved, even if this for example seems to other worried people to be of absolutely no consequence. If then, with the movement of the bird to and fro, comparison has worked up our worries to a passion, and got the worried one torn loose from the soil, that is, from willing to be what he was intended to be, then it seems for a moment as if comparison had now come to fetch the worried one to his desired goal. And come to fetch him it certainly does, but only as when death fetches a man. For it allows the worried one to die on the fluttering wings of despondency. [VIII. pp. 300 f.; CL pp. 21 ff.]

PRAYER

Father in heaven! From thee cometh only a good and perfect gift. Whomsoever thou dost vouchsafe to appoint as a teacher of men, as a guide to those who are worried, such a person's guidance and teaching it must indeed be profitable to follow. Grant then thy grace to those who are worried, that they may learn of those divinely appointed teachers, of the lilies of the field and the birds of the heaven! Amen. [VIII. p. 290; CL p. 11.]

THE GLORY OF MANHOOD: A PARABLE — II

If we cannot, without a smile, think about the lily's anxiety to become a crown imperial, think of it dying on the way, then let us on the other hand reflect how sad it is, when a person is worried equally unreasonably. Equally unreasonably? Yet no. How dare I let that sentence stand? How dare I take upon myself to judge these divinely appointed teachers, the lilies of the field? No, the lily is *not* worried in the way I said, and that is precisely why we should learn from them. And when therefore a man, like the lily, is content with being a man, then he does not make himself ill through temporal worries. And if temporal worries do not worry him, then he remains firm in the place appointed him; and if he remains there, then it is true that by being man he is more glorious than the glory of Solomon.

For what does the worried one learn of the lilies? He learns to be content with being man and not to be worried by the difference between man and man. He learns to speak just as concisely, just as ceremoniously, just as sublimely, about what it is to be a man, as the gospel speaks concisely about the lilies. For it is certainly men's usual custom, on occasions of great ceremony, to speak in ceremonial fashion. Let us think of Solomon. When he puts on his royal purple, when he is enthroned majestically in all his glory, then, indeed, ceremonious speech is appropriate. We say, "Your Majesty."

But when in the earnest speech of eternity he is to be addressed in the most ceremonial way possible, then we call him "man." And we say exactly the same to the humblest, even if, like Lazarus, he lies all but unrecognized, in poverty and misery. We call him "man." And in the decisive moment of death, when all differences are put away, we say "man." And in saying this we are not speaking depreciatingly. On the contrary we are using the highest of expressions. For to be a man is not something lower than the differences. It is elevated above them. Nor is this essentially equal glory among all men to be regarded as in the least like the dismal equality of death; any more than is the essential likeness among all the lilies. On the contrary, that is a likeness in loveliness.

All *worldly* anxiety has its ground in the fact that a man will not be content with being a man, and also in the fact that anxious craving is directed, by comparison, toward difference. We dare not, on the other hand, say straight out, and without further ado, that *earthly* and *temporal* anxiety is the discovery of comparison. For a man does not, when need is upon him, discover by comparison that he requires food and clothing. Even he who lived alone among the lilies of the field, and had no opportunity of comparison, he too would discover this need. Care for the necessity, or (to use the dismal plural we usually do) the necessities, of life, is not simply the discovery of comparison; though it is a question whether comparison does not, in innumerable ways, ambiguously help to decide what should be understood by " necessity." . . . May we not learn much about this also, from the lilies and the birds? [VIII. pp. 303 f.; CL pp. 24 f.]

PRAYER

Father in heaven! From thee comes only a good and perfect gift. Whomsoever thou dost vouchsafe to appoint as a teacher of men, as a guide to those who are worried, such a person's guidance and teaching it must indeed be profitable to follow. Grant then thy grace to those who are worried, that they may learn of those divinely appointed teachers, of the lilies of the field and the birds of the heavens! Amen. [VIII. p. 290; CL p. 11.]

ANXIETY ABOUT SUBSISTENCE — I

Behold the fowls of the air: for they sow not, neither do they reap, nor gather into barns; yet your heavenly Father feedeth them. Are ye not much better than they? (*Matt. 6:26.*)

There was once a wood pigeon. In the frowning wood, where wonder and agitation dwell together, among the erect, lonely tree trunks, this wood pigeon had its nest. But nearby, where the smoke rises up from the farmer's house, dwelt some tame pigeons. The wood pigeon would often meet a pair of these. He would sit on a branch which spread out over the farm, and they on the ridge of the roof. One day they were talking together about subsistence. The wood pigeon said, "I let every day have its own troubles, and so I get through life." The tame pigeon, not without preening itself, answered: "With us — that is to say, with the rich farmer with whom we live — it is different. The future is secure. At harvesttime the farmer drives in so many loads of corn that I know we are secure for a long time. We two have our guaranteed security."

When the wood pigeon returned home, he reflected closely on the matter. Immediately it occurred to him that it must be a great comfort to *know* that one's subsistence was secure for a long time, and on the contrary what a wretched thing it was to have to live always in such uncertainty. "It would be best," he told himself, "if you gathered in a great store, which you could put in some secure place."

Next morning he wakened earlier than usual, and was so busy gathering that he scarcely had time to eat. But it was as if a fate hung over him, for every time he had collected a little store and concealed it, when he came to look for it it was gone! Meantime there was no actual change in regard to his subsistence. He found his food every day as before. And yet a great change had taken place. He did not suffer actual want, but he had an *anticipation* of want in the future. His peace had gone. He had discovered *anxiety* about the necessities of life.

From now on, the wood pigeon began to be anxious. His feathers lost their glint of color, his flight its lightness. He was joyous no more; indeed, he was almost envious of the rich pigeons. He found his food each day, and yet he was not satisfied. In worrying about his needs he went hungry for a long time. He had caught himself in a trap in which no birdcatcher could have caught him, a trap in which only a free creature can catch himself. "This securing of the future is constantly in my mind," he said. "O why am I a poor wood pigeon and not one of the rich ones?"

He saw plainly that care was telling on him, and he spoke seriously to himself, yet not so seriously that he could drive the worry from his mind and set his heart at rest; but he spoke in such a way that he convinced himself that his care was justified. "I am not asking anything unreasonable or impossible," he said. "I do not ask to become like the rich farmer, but only like one of the rich pigeons."

At last he thought of a stratagem. One day he flew off and sat on the ridge beam of the farmer's roof, between the tame pigeons. He noticed a place where they flew in, so he flew in too, for there, no doubt, was the storehouse. But when the farmer came home in the evening and closed the pigeon loft, he discovered the strange pigeon. He straightway put it in a little compartment by itself till the next day, when it was killed — and released from worry about necessities of life! Alas, the wood pigeon had not only entrapped itself in worry, but also in the pigeon loft — to its death! [VIII. p. 308 f. ab; CL p. 29 f.]

PRAYER

Father in heaven! From thee comes only a good and perfect gift. Whomsoever thou dost vouchsafe to appoint as a teacher of men, as a guide to those who are worried, such a person's guidance and teaching it must indeed be profitable to follow. Grant then thy grace to those who are worried, that they may learn of those divinely appointed teachers, of the lilies of the field and the birds of the heavens! Amen. [VIII. p. 290; CL p. 11.]

ANXIETY ABOUT SUBSISTENCE — II

Behold the fowls of the air. (Matt. 6:26.)

That wood pigeon is man. Yet no, it is only my speech that has allowed the wood pigeon to be treated in this way, the bird taking all the blame. And the pigeon has willingly consented, because it knows right well that it is one of the divinely appointed teachers from whom we are to learn. A teacher does sometimes act like this. He exhibits in himself the very wrong he would fain warn us against.

The wood pigeon then is man. When a man is content with the dignity of being a man, then he understands that his Heavenly Father feeds him, and this he learns from the bird of heaven. He lives not only like the tame birds in the house of the rich farmer, but in the house of Him who is richer than all. For since heaven and earth are the house and possession of God, man is his guest.

This means that a man must be content to be a dependent being, as little capable of sustaining himself as of creating himself. But if a man chooses to forget God, and look after his own sustenance, then he involves himself in anxiety. No doubt it is a praiseworthy thing and well-pleasing to God, that a man should toil for his food. But should he forget God, and think he is supporting himself, then he involves himself in anxiety about the necessities of life. If the richest man that ever lived forgets God, and thinks he is supporting himself, he has this carking anxiety. Let us not stupidly and small-mindedly say that the rich man is spared this anxiety, while the poor man is not. On the contrary, only he is spared who is content with being a man, and understands that his Heavenly Father feeds him. And this is as possible for a rich man as for a poor man.

No external power, no *actual* circumstance, can take a man in this snare. If he chooses to be his own providence, then he goes quite *ingenuously* into the trap, the rich man quite as easily as the poor man. If he ensconce himself into his own plot of ground which is not to be under God's providence, then he is living, though he marks it not, in a prison. Like the farmer shutting the door on the pigeon, he believes he is now safe, when in fact he is caught; or to put it another way, he is shut out from the care of Providence and handed over to carking anxiety. And in a spiritual sense he has made himself captive — to death. [VIII. p. 311 f. ab, ad; CL p. 31 f.]

PRAYER

Father in heaven! From thee cometh only a good and perfect gift. Whomsoever thou dost vouchsafe to appoint as a teacher of men, as a guide to those who are worried, such a person's guidance and teaching it must indeed be profitable to follow. Grant then thy grace to those who are worried, that they may learn of those divinely appointed teachers, of the lilies of the field and the birds of the heavens! Amen. [VIII. p. 290; CL p. 11.]

"KNOCK, AND IT SHALL BE OPENED"

Ask, and it shall be given you; seek, and ye shall find; knock, and it shall be opened unto you: for every one that asketh receiveth; and he that seeketh findeth; and to him that knocketh it shall be opened. (Matt. 7:7, 8.)

He who knocks — to him shall it be opened. And even if God does not immediately open, be comforted. Imagine an older person who sat in his room making some preparations to please a child who is to visit him at a certain time. But the child came too early. He knocked, but it was not opened to him. The child could see that there was somebody in the room, because there was a light. The child's knocking therefore was certainly heard; and yet the door was not opened.

So the child became disconsolate. Ah, but why was not the door opened? Because the preparations for the child's happiness were not yet quite finished. [VIII. 586.]

" Knock and it shall be opened unto you." It is then eternally certain that when anybody knocks, it is opened to him. Ah, but suppose the difficulty for us men is that we are afraid to go and knock!

Believe; and if you bid it do so, the mountain shall be lifted up and cast into the sea. It is then eternally certain that this is so. Ah, but suppose the difficulty for us men consists in the very fact that we cannot help being anxious and afraid of having such enormous strength that we *want* the mountain to be lifted up. . . . But then it might fall on me! [1] [X⁴. A. 455.]

PRAYER
Whatever happens, and however things may go, I hope in God that this may be vouchsafed to me: May my last words be, when I have for the last time repented me of my sin and received the forgiveness of my sins through the fullness of his grace — may my last words be as I die, that I thank God for the indescribable goodness he has shown toward me — far more than I could have ever expected. This is indeed eternally true. For what I suffer ei-

[1] In the last paragraph, the change from " us men " to " me " is suggestive. Kierkegaard was thinking of how he felt called to overturn the mountain of official Christianity. The thought of this must often have made him anxious lest he should be himself crushed by the fall of so great a colossus. But still he did not shrink from what he felt convinced was his duty. Nor should we.

ther has its basis in my sin and sins or else it is precisely because God has done so extremely much for me. The result of his goodness cannot in this world be other than we have to suffer for it. But for this very reason it is entirely certain and true that God has done exceeding great things for us. [IX. A. 371.]

PART
III

SOME BIBLICAL PERSONALITIES

NICODEMUS — I: FEAR, FORMALITY, AND FALSE PREACHING

There was a man of the Pharisees, named Nicodemus, a ruler
of the Jews: the same came to Jesus by night. (John 3:1, 2.)

The woman that was a sinner, though both woman and sinner,
dared to go into the Pharisee's house to find Christ, where the
Pharisees were assembled for a banquet. Nicodemus, though he
regarded himself as a righteous man, only dared to come to Jesus
at night. [X². A. 29; J 968.]

1. We come to Christ, concealed not by night, but by something that possibly hides us even better — self-delusion. The
whole of our Christianity can be a delusion wherein we hide ourselves; and yet we can still live in the delusion that we openly
come to Christ by day, e.g., that because we are baptized as children, confirmed as children, etc., we prove that we are Christians. This is sheer delusion.

2. In so-called Christian countries we have removed any danger involved in confessing Christ. But we may also have put out
of sight the fact that we can only confess Christ truly in our lives,
openly. To omit this latter — is it not, once more, like Nicodemus,
to come to Christ by night? God is Spirit. He cannot therefore be
worshiped in truth by poems (even though they were masterpieces) or by speeches (even though they were masterpieces).
Such a thing is like a cake and sweetmeats to God, and it pleases
him not. No, if you want to adore God in truth, then it must be
by deeds [and not words only]. Of course you must not then become self-important, and imagine that your deeds have any
merit in themselves, for that sort of worship is loathsome to God.
But deeds and actions, these are the sacrifices which must be
brought to God in humility and faith. So also with confession of
Christ, by deeds. Your life must confess him. But if it does, dan-

ger will come. Look! this danger is abolished in " Christendom."
Is not this then, à la Nicodemus, to come to Christ by night?

For what does " by night" really mean? It means that we want
to have danger removed. Concealed we will be with Christ, like
Nicodemus, yes . . . we will keep with Christ in "hidden inwardness." [1] Whether we do keep with Christ, I do not know, but
if we do, then being in " hidden " inwardness makes us like Nicodemus; not a whit better, indeed worse, because he was only a
single man. The Nicodemus element has now become established.
O what depth of confusion! Nicodemus must at least suffer because he sees what a sneak he was to come by night, but we ex-
pose ourselves to no such suffering. [E.P. VIII. 146 ad.]

PRAYER

Lord Jesus Christ, that we may be able rightly to pray for all
things, we pray first for one: Help us to love thee much; increase
love and inflame it. And be thou the perfect love which casteth
out fear. [XI. p. 303; CD p. 379.]

NICODEMUS — II: ADMIRATION
OR IMITATION?

*This is the condemnation, that light is come into the world,
and men loved darkness rather than light. (John 3:19.)*

Anybody who has any knowledge of men, and is not put off
from being honest, either by regard for wealth or fear of men,
must concede unconditionally that a Nicodemus in every age is a
great rarity. When danger is seriously afoot, and one is, like Nicodemus, a person of distinction, and the danger one faces is insult,

[1] In Denmark and elsewhere there was, and is, much talk to the effect
that " religion is a private affair, something between the soul and God
only."

mockery, and ejection from society, then how few there are who feel sufficiently for the truth to determine to go out at night and get into touch with such truth. There are very, very few distinguished people in any age who will do this — perhaps only an isolated individual. For just because such people are distinguished, they have so much to lose. Nicodemus was an admirer. To face danger in actual life was too much for him. Personally he wished to keep out of it. On the other hand, truth concerned him so much that he sought to come to terms with it. Concealed by night, (for he was treading forbidden paths), he stole out to the despised Truth. It had indeed cost him a lot to make this venture of seeking the society of the despised One. . . .

Yet there is something despicable in being such an admirer. Not that I or any average person would be justified in saying this of Nicodemus as though we were any better. It is rather Nicodemus who is able to judge *us*. But we see here what an admirer really is; for Nicodemus never became an imitator. It is as if Nicodemus had said to Christ: "If only we could come to an agreement whereby I may accept thy teaching in eternity! But not in this world. No, that I cannot do. Could you not make an exception of me? Would it not be enough if I come to you once in a while by night? But by day — oh, I confess how humiliating this is for me, how it puts me to shame; and indeed how insulting it is toward you also — by day I know you not. By day I say, 'I know not the man.'"

See here in what a web of untruth an admirer entangles himself.

If Christ had permitted a cheaper edition of what it is to imitate him; if he had permitted a person to be an admirer who protests by all that is high and holy that he is convinced, then Nicodemus would have been eligible. But there is an infinite difference between an admirer and an imitator; for an imitator is, or strives to be, what he admires. The imitator, in order to be an imitator, must venture his life, his all.

But suppose it be true that there is nowadays no danger involved in confessing Christ — this does not mean that the distinction admiration/imitation is unrecognizable. Think of the danger in actual life today which is unavoidably connected with being a Christian. Does not Christianity contain instruction about morality and duty? Does it not demand that we should die from the world, renounce what is earthly, and exercise self-denial? Does not this contain demands enough which, if they are to be complied with, could produce danger in real life such as makes the difference between an "admirer" and an "imitator" obvious? makes it obvious by the very fact that the imitator has his life fixed in these dangers, while the admirer keeps himself aloof, even though they are both agreed in words to recognize the truth of Christianity? [XII. p. 272 ff.; TC p. 241 ff.]

We read about that ruler, member of the Sanhedrin, that he went to Christ by night. Now you must not divert your attention by saying, with some apparent show of right, that it was odd of him to choose such a time! What good is it to want to be concealed, and to choose to go by night, when the Person you go to is *Light?* If I say, "the darkness shall cover me, then shall my night be turned to day." [1] No, you must not talk like that, for you know well enough why Nicodemus chose the night. . . .

When you read about Nicodemus, about him upon whom Christ had indeed made an impression, yet only to the extent that he could neither quite surrender himself nor tear himself away, so that he chose the night, chose to steal to Christ in the night — then you must say to yourself, "It is I." Do not seek evasions, do not introduce irrelevancies, do not say: "He was one of the people of rank, and people of rank are like that, great for their rank, and yet so cowardly and faithless. How can the gospel, which is for the poor, be for people of rank?" No. You must not talk like that. When you read God's Word you have nothing to do with people of rank, or with rank in general, or with arraigning them. For if you yourself were one of these people of rank, you still have to do only with yourself. No, you must say, "It is I."

It is I who would seek evasions. I who would once again con-

[1] Cf. Ps. 139:11.

ceal myself in the darkness of the night, however little it avails
when I stand before One who is Light. It is I who would conceal
myself in evasion or excuse, as though I had not understood God's
Word, as though it were only people of rank that the gospel
speaks about. No, it was I. O how could I be so paltry, such a
wretch, neither hot nor cold, neither one thing nor the other!
[XII. pp. 380 f.; FSE pp. 66 f.]

PRAYER
Lord, teach me, reveal to me, how much I need repentance.
Let me experience what the natural man may not notice. Even
when I do not feel like it, may I think upon thee. When I feel
cold and far away from thee, then also may I think upon thee, and
pray thee to help me think upon thee. And may I never be offended! [IX. A. 322 ad.]

ABRAHAM — I: HIS CONFIDENCE
AND RESIGNATION

*And it came to pass after these things, that God did tempt
Abraham, and said unto him, Abraham: and he said, Behold,
here I am. And he said, Take now thy son, thine only son Isaac,
whom thou lovest, and get thee into the land of Moriah; and
offer him there for a burnt offering upon one of the mountains
which I will tell thee of.*

*And Abraham rose up early in the morning, and saddled his
ass, and took two of his young men with him, and Isaac his son,
and clave the wood for the burnt offering, and rose up, and went
unto the place of which God had told him. Then on the third
day Abraham lifted up his eyes, and saw the place afar off. And
Abraham said unto his young men, Abide ye here with the ass;
and I and the lad will go yonder and worship, and come again to
you. And Abraham took the wood of the burnt offering, and laid
it upon Isaac his son; and took the fire in his hand, and a knife;
and they went both of them together. (Gen. 22:1–6.)*

It is this confident, resigned attitude in Abraham; this fearlessness in going to meet his trials; this dauntless answer, "Here am I," that we must specially notice.

Is it the same with us? Or is it not rather that when we observe hard trials approaching, we usually want to withdraw? We only wanted a remote corner of the world in which to conceal ourselves. We wished that a mountain would cover us, or we impatiently seek to pass the burden over from ourselves to others. Or even those who do not seek to flee, how slowly, how reluctantly their foot moves forward on the way! Not so with Abraham. He dauntlessly answers, "Here am I." He troubles nobody about his sufferings; not Sarah, who, he perceived, would be so sorely afflicted in losing Isaac; not Eliezer, the faithful servant in his house, in whom, if anybody, he might have sought comfort.

We read, "He rose up early in the morning." He hastened as to a festival of joy, and with the dawn he was at the place prescribed by the Lord, namely, at Mt. Moriah.

And he clave the wood, bound Isaac, kindled the fire, and drew the knife. . . . There were many fathers in Israel who believed that in losing their child they lost everything that was dear to them, that they were bereft of every future hope. But there was no one who was the child of promise in the same sense as Isaac was for Abraham. There were many fathers who lost their child, but that, they said, was due to God's almighty and unsearchable governance. It was God who himself, as it were, deleted the promise he had given. The father must say like Job, "The Lord gave and the Lord took." Not so Abraham. It was upon his own hand that the demand was made. Isaac's fate was laid, with the knife, in Abraham's hand. And he stood early on the mountain — he, the old man, with his only hope.

But he doubted not. He did not look round to the right or to the left. He did not besiege heaven with complaints. He knew it was the heaviest sacrifice God could demand, but he knew also that nothing was too great for God.

We all know what was the outcome of the story. Perhaps it no longer surprises us, because we have known it from our earliest childhood. But in that case the fault truly does not lie in the story, but in us, because we are too lukewarm rightly to feel with Abraham and to suffer with him.

He went home happy, fearless, resigned to God. Because he had not wavered, he had nothing to reproach himself for. If we want to imagine that Abraham, by looking round in agony and despair, had discovered the ram which was to save his son, then would he not have returned home ashamed, without confidence for the future, without the certainty in his heart that he had been ready to bring to God any offering whatsoever that God demanded, without that celestial voice from heaven in his heart which spoke to him of God's grace and love?

Nor did Abraham say: " Now I am an old man. My youth went by, and my dream was not fulfilled. I became a man, and what I desired thou didst deny me. Then I became an old man, and in a wonderful way thou didst fulfill everything. Grant me now a quiet eventide. Call me not forth again to a new struggle. Let me rejoice in what thou gavest me, the comfort of my old age." [III. C. 4.]

He who spared Abraham's first-born, and only made trial of the patriarch's faith — he spared not his only begotten Son. [II. A. 569.]

PRAYER

O Heavenly Father, when in the hour of sorrow we would strengthen and encourage our hearts with the thought of those great men, thy chosen instruments, who in sharp trials and anxiety of heart kept their souls free, their courage unbroken, and the heavens open, then will we add our witness of thy love to theirs, in the conviction that though our courage is but despondency in comparison with theirs, our strength but weakness, yet thou art the same, the same mighty God who tries our spirits in combat, the same Father without whose will not a sparrow falls to the earth. Amen. [III. p. 19; ED I. p. 6.]

ABRAHAM — II: THE COLLISION

And it came to pass after these things, that God did tempt Abraham, and said unto him, Abraham: and he said, Behold, here I am. (Gen. 22:1.)

Let us suppose (a thing which neither the Old Testament nor the Koran tells us) that Isaac knew that the purpose of the journey he was to take with his father to Mt. Moriah, was that he should be sacrificed. If there were a poet living today, he would be able to tell us what the conversation between these two men would be on the way. I picture Abraham looking with all his fatherly love upon Isaac. His venerable countenance and his broken heart made his speech more forceful. He exhorted Isaac to bear his fate with patience, let him darkly understand that he as father suffers more than Isaac in all this. But it was of no avail.

I then imagine Abraham turning for a moment away from Isaac, and when he again turned toward him, he was unrecognizable. His eye was wild, his aspect freezing. His venerable locks were lifted like the Furies over his head. He seized Isaac by the breast, he drew the knife, he said: "You thought it was for God's sake I wanted to do this; but you were wrong. I am an idolator. The passion of idolatry has once more awakened in my soul: to murder you — that is my desire. I am worse than any cannibal. Despair, foolish boy, who imagined that I was your father. I am your murderer, and that is my desire." And Isaac fell upon his knee and called to heaven, "Merciful God, have pity on me." But Abraham then said quite softly to himself: "This is as it should be. For it is better that he believes me to be an inhuman monster; that he curse me for being his father, and yet can still pray to God. Better this than that he should know that it was God who laid this trial on me. For then he would lose his understanding and perhaps curse God."

But where is the poet of today who could suspect such collisions as these? And yet Abraham's conduct was genuinely poetical and high-minded — more high-minded than anything I have
read of in tragedies.

When the child must be weaned, the mother blackens her
breast. But her eye rests just as lovingly upon the child, who
thinks that it is the breast that has changed, though in fact the
mother is unchanged. And why does she blacken her breast? Because she thinks it a shame that her breast should look so attrac-
tive when the child may not have it.

Here is a collision that is easily resolved, because the breast is
only a part of the mother herself. Happy the man who has not
experienced more dreadful collisions, who has not needed to
blacken himself, who has not needed to journey to hell in order to
find out how a devil looks, so that he could delineate himself like
one, and if possible save another person by doing so — at least in
that person's attitude to God. That would be an Abraham-colli-
sion.[1] [IV. A. 76.]

PRAYER

O God, men think the heroes of tragedy great, and they admire
them. But Abraham's contemporaries could not understand him.
What then did he achieve? That he was true to his love. And he
who loves God has no need of admiration, no need that others
weep for him. He forgets his suffering in love, forgets it so thor-
oughly that no one even suspects his pain except thee, O God,
who seest in secret, and knowest the need, and countest the tears
and forgettest nothing. [III. 184 ad; FT 187.]

[1] Kierkegaard bases his book *Fear and Trembling* very largely on the
theme of Abraham, and in it he develops his own views of Faith and
Paradox, and of the relationship between ethics and religion. The
above passage, written in 1843 (*Fear and Trembling* came out in Octo-
ber of that year), can almost be said to be a preliminary casting of the
first of the four sections in *Fear and Trembling*, bearing the general
title " Prelude."

ABRAHAM — III: HIS CONSTANCY

And the Angel of the Lord called unto him out of heaven, and said, Abraham, Abraham: and he said, Here am I. And he said, Lay not thine hand upon the lad, neither do thou any thing unto him: for now I know that thou fearest God, seeing thou hast not withheld thy son, thine only son, from me. (Gen. 22:11, 12.)

A PICTURE: HOW IT MIGHT HAVE BEEN WITH ABRAHAM

"FEAR AND TREMBLING"

. . . And he clave the wood, he bound Isaac, he lighted the fire, he drew the knife, he thrust it into Isaac!

At that instant Jehovah stood by Abraham's side in bodily form and said: "What hast thou done? O wretched old man! That was not asked of you at all. You are my friend, I only wanted to try your faith! I called to you at the last moment. I cried, 'Abraham, Abraham, refrain!'"

Then answered Abraham with a voice whose feebleness betokened half mystic adoration and half the disheveled feebleness which belongs to mental derangement: "O Lord, I did not hear. Yet now thou dost speak of it, I seem to remember that I did hear such a voice. O when it is thou, my God, who commandest, when it is thou who commandest a father to murder his own child, then a man at such a time is under some strain. Hence I did not hear thy voice. And if I had heard it, dared I have believed it was thine? If thou commandest me to sacrifice my child, and then at the decisive moment a voice is heard saying, 'Refrain,' then I am obliged to believe it is the voice of the Tempter which would keep me back from fulfilling thy will. One of two things: either I ought to have assumed that the voice that said to me, 'Sacrifice Isaac,' was the Tempter's voice, and then I should not have sallied forth. But when I had assured myself that it was thy voice, then I must conclude that this other voice was the Tempter's."

So Abraham went home; and the Lord gave him a new Isaac. But Abraham did not look upon him with any joy. When he looked upon him he shook his head and said, " This was not my Isaac."

But to Sarah he said: " It was very strange. That it was God's demand that I should offer Isaac is certain, eternally certain. God himself cannot disavow that. Yet when I took it seriously, it was a mistake on my part. It was not God's will."

The Truth: How in Fact It Was with Abraham

But it did not go like that with Abraham, the father of faith. His obedience lies just in the fact that at the very last moment he immediately and unreservedly obeyed as he did. For oh! when a man has for a long time been saying " A," then, humanly speaking, he is very inclined to be offended at having to say " B." It is harder, when one has actually drawn the knife, to be able and willing, with implicit obedience, to recognize that after all no demand is made, than it is to set forth to Mt. Moriah with the purpose of offering Isaac. Compared with deciding whether to sacrifice one's only child or to spare him, oh, it is *great* to retain, even at the last moment, the obedient, and, if I may venture to say so, the agile willingness of a servingman, who, even when he has almost reached his goal, does not mind having to run back again, thereby rendering all his running in vain. Oh, this is great! " No one was so great as Abraham — who can comprehend him? " [X⁴. A. 338.]

Prayer

Teach me, Lord, that the fight of faith is not a fight with doubt, thought against thought, but a fight for character. Enable me to see that human vanity consists in wanting to understand. Save me from the vanity of not being willing to obey like a child, and of wanting to be like a grown man who can understand. Help me to realize that he who will not obey when he cannot understand does not, in any essential sense, obey thee at all.

Make me a believer, a " character man," who, unreservedly

obedient, sees it as necessary for his character's sake that he must be unable to understand. Make me willing to believe what I cannot understand and to stand firm when such blind obedience is called obscurantism, and folly. Let not the world tempt me with human fear to become so vain as to think I can understand; for that were to fear men more than thee. [X¹. A. 367 ad.]

JOB — I: AGAINST GOD WE ARE ALWAYS IN THE WRONG

If I justify myself, mine own mouth shall condemn me: if I say, I am perfect, it shall also prove me perverse. (Job 9:20.)

Job says rightly that even if he were in the right, he could never be in the right toward God, because he would become nervous before the Judge.[1] [X¹. A. 196.]

For God's thoughts are eternally higher than human thoughts, and therefore all human ideas about torture and misfortune, about what is joyful and what sorrowful, are erroneous thoughts. By remaining within the ambit of these human ideas, a man always remains in the wrong before God; and only escapes from this circle of false ideas by recognizing that toward God he is always in the wrong. When, for example, impatience begins to stir in the heart of one who, humanly speaking, is suffering innocently, as Job did; when impatience moves the heart of one whom God is testing as he tested Job; when such a man wants in some way to be in the right toward God, because, humanly speaking, he is in the right about this or that — what then? Is he to be permitted to, or *can* he, reverse the relationship toward God? (For this *is* a reversed relationship, because a man in fact is always in the wrong

[1] For this sentence Kierkegaard refers us to the text quoted above (Job 9:20), which in the Bible of his day ran: "though I were righteous, my mouth would yet judge me to be unrighteous. Though I were free from guilt, God would then pervert my cause."

against God. Therefore all is reversed if ever he is in the right toward God, though it be only for a moment and in the very smallest matter.) Shall the one who doubts be in the right or, what is the same thing, is everything to be lost? No, for then something else happens. The one on trial knows that instead of speaking to others, he must speak by himself with God; and we others know that out of respect for him we dare not say more; dare not hold him guilty. This makes the final reinforcement advance into the battle: "In relation to God, a man suffers because he is always guilty," is the battle cry. But no. The basic relationship between God and man is that a man is a sinner, and God is the Holy One. Over against God a man is not a sinner in this or that, but is *essentially* a sinner; not guilty in this or that, but essentially and unconditionally guilty. But if he is essentially guilty, then he is *always* guilty; therefore the debt of essential guilt is so deep that it makes all direct accounting impossible. Between man and man the position is that a man may be right in this and wrong in that. But such a position between God and any man is impossible, because if that were the position, then God would not be God, but a man's equal; and again if that were the position, the guilt would not be essential guilt. [VIII. 429 f.; GS p. 91.]

PRAYER

Father, I could not wish that it were otherwise. I cannot wish that *I* should be in the right, and not thee. For then were everything lost. I cannot wish that the beautiful law which for thousands of years has supported the race throughout its life, supported every generation of the human race, that beautiful law, more glorious than the law which supports the stars in their courses over the vault of heaven — I cannot wish that this law should burst. For that were more dreadful than if that law of nature were to lose its force and everything be dissolved into an appalling chaos.[1] [II. p. 380; EO p. 293 ad.]

[1] Kierkegaard asks questions. Could we wish things different, etc.? I have adapted the questions by answering no to them before God in prayer, saying, "I could not wish things different."

JOB — II: MISCELLANEOUS THOUGHTS

And the Lord said unto Satan, Whence comest thou? Then Satan answered the Lord, and said, From going to and fro in the earth, and from walking up and down in it. (Job 1:7.)

We read in The Book of Job that Satan came to earth to reconnoiter, and walk to and fro. This indicates that there is a kind of observing which has the nature of evil, as indeed it usually has when it is due to mere curiosity. [X¹. A. 193.]

> *Now when Job's three friends heard of all this evil that was come upon him, they came every one from his own place; Eliphaz the Temanite, and Bildad the Shuhite, and Zophar the Naamathite: for they had made an appointment together to come to mourn with him, and to comfort him. (Job 2:11.)*
>
> *So these three men ceased to answer Job, because he was righteous in his own eyes. Then was kindled the wrath of Elihu the son of Barachel the Buzite, of the kindred of Ram: against Job was his wrath kindled, . . . because they had found no answer, and yet had condemned Job. Now Elihu had waited till Job had spoken, because they were elder than he. (Job 32:1–4.)*

When the three friends (who were elder men) had become, as it were, tired of answering Job, or had lost patience with him, and I suppose were not far from conceding that he was right, then begins the young man Elihu.

We may understand this as follows. The ideality of faith is in one sense represented most truly, i.e., most ideally, in the young man, because as yet he lacks experience. The elder man, the experienced man — ah, it all too easily happens to him that his faith has suffered a little damage! He is therefore more inclined to bargain, to "knock a bit off," as we say, while youth still retains its pure ideality. [X⁴. A. 146.]

The significance of The Book of Job is really to show the cruelty which we men perpetrate by regarding misfortune as due to some guilt or crime. This is human selfishness, which wishes to avoid the feeling — the serious and harrowing feeling — which suffering impresses upon us when we see what terrible things can happen to a man in this life. In order to fortify themselves against such impressions, men explain suffering as guilt. "It is his own fault," they say. Oh, human cruelty!

That which concerns Job is to justify himself — and in a sense in the sight of God, but above all in the sight of his friends, who, instead of comforting him, martyr him with the supposition that he suffers because he is guilty. [X⁴. A. 396; J 1233.]

Though he slay me, yet will I trust in him. (Job 13:15.)

Thou, Lord, didst allow all to go well with me. Then there came a time when I felt as if thou didst allow all to go ill with me. I understood this as indicating that all was over, and that in that sense thou wouldst have nothing more to do with me. Then I reflected that there was anyway one bliss left for me, uninterruptedly to thank thee for the indescribable good thou hadst shown toward me; so infinitely more than I could or dared have expected. Oh, how petty was my heart, which in spite of everything, could think so meanly of thee! No, thy purpose was that I should make progress; and that through the indescribable good thou hast shown toward me (shown me in such a way that I could understand it) I might learn the blessedness of praising and thanking thee when I cannot understand anything — except that everything is going badly for me. [X³. A. 222.]

THE WOMAN WHO ANOINTED
CHRIST'S HEAD

Now when Jesus was in Bethany, in the house of Simon the leper, there came unto him a woman having an alabaster box of very precious ointment, and poured it on his head, as he sat at meat. (Matt. 26:6, 7.)

Relationship to God is the only thing that imparts significance. This we see pre-eminently in Christ's life. Here was a day, a day which probably had had its eventfulness, and everybody had spoken of this as being of immense importance — on this eventful day a woman anointed Christ's head. How insignificant — compared with the other events! Yet all else is now forgotten, and only she remembered. Yet never I think did the divine dignity, and the consciousness of being God, come out more strongly in Christ's life (not even when he performed a miracle) than it does here. For here he displays the infinite *reality* of his life, that such an insignificant event is worthy to be eternally remembered; an unknown woman, an infinitesimal nothing, becomes immortal, merely because she one day anointed his head. [VIII. A. 670; J 759.]

PRAYER

Father in heaven! Thou who carest for the sparrow — not in such a cruel way as to demand of the sparrow that it should be as thou art; no, thou dost lovingly care for the sparrow in such a way that with fatherly care thou puttest thyself in its place — thou carest also for man. And if thou dost demand of him that he strive to be like thee (a thing thou canst not demand of the sparrow), thou dost not demand this of him cruelly. No, with fatherly care thou dost put thyself in his place, and thou thyself art he who givest strength to strive. [X². A. 342.]

PETER: PENITENCE, OR OFFENSE?

From that time many of his disciples went back, and walked no more with him. Then said Jesus unto the twelve, Will ye also go away? Then Simon Peter answered him, Lord, to whom shall we go? thou hast the words of eternal life. (John 6:66–68.)

He rose again the third day . . . and . . . was seen of Cephas. (I Cor. 15:4, 5.)

I understand the words of Peter, " To whom shall we go? " to refer to his consciousness of sin. It is this that binds a man to Christianity. And, since it is God, who, through the consciousness of sin, binds every individual person to Christianity, so it must be assumed that he also determines every man's conflicts individually. Hence the consciousness of sin is ever the force that binds a man to Christianity. Every one who is not so bound is not Christianly bound. . . . This is the situation: — if I were not conscious of being a sinner, I must be offended at Christianity. But the consciousness of sin stops my mouth, and in spite of the possibility of offense, I choose to believe in Christianity. The thing is as profound as that. Christianity repels in order to attract. [IX. A. 310; J 820.]

How Peter must have suffered in those three days when Christ was dead! To be parted from Christ in this way, after having denied him. How dreadful! And yet he was not cast off, but received by grace, so that he became what he did — an apostle. See what indescribable lenience this is, compared with Jehovah's attitude toward Moses. Merely because Moses at one time doubted, he was not allowed to come into the Promised Land.[1]

O infinite lenience! I am almost afraid that it may beguile me, so that I take it in vain. [X³. A. 149.]

[1] Cf. Num. 20:12.

PRAYER

Whither should we turn, if not to thee, Lord Jesus Christ? Where might the sufferer find consolation, if not in thee? Ah! and where the penitent if not in thee, Lord Jesus Christ? [XI. p. 281; CD p. 361.]

Father in heaven, open thou the springs of mine eyes; let a stream of tears like another Flood wipe out all my past life which has not found grace in thy sight. But do thou also give a sign as aforetime, when thou didst set the rainbow like a portal of grace upon the heavens — give a sign that thou wilt never more wipe us out with such a Flood. Let not sin ever get such power over us that thou must rend us out of this body of sin. [II. A. 342; J 257.]

PART IV

PARABLES AND MIRACLES OF JESUS

THE PARABLE OF THE POUNDS

He called his ten servants, and delivered them ten pounds.
(Luke 19:13.)

Perhaps you say: " Happy the man to whom it was vouchsafed to be faithful over little. But as for me, nothing at all was given me to work with, because the pound which was entrusted to me was not a force to work with, but a weight, a burden which was laid on my shoulders." It is, however, rarely that a man can with truth speak like this. But if you bear this burden with humility, if you were to lose all the world without taking any harm to your soul, if you loved God, if even your sorrowful life sometimes was transfigured by thankfulness, if you believed in God and in the depth of the riches both of his wisdom and knowledge — and if you dared to lift up unspotted hands to God, if this burden which you richly deserved rested still more heavily upon you, if you yet humbled yourself under God's powerful hand, did not complain, did not follow the world's " wise " advice to forget, did not presume to say, " Are my sufferings never to cease? "; if you loved God in your sorrow — were you not then " faithful over a little "? [III. A. 182.]

Of the servants who each received his pound when the nobleman went into a far country, one immediately went and concealed it in the earth. The mistake straightway was that he produced an appearance, an illusion. He, I mean, who chooses to work with his pound at that moment takes a risk with it. Only later does it appear whether he has gained anything or whether he has lost his pound. He who conceals it in the earth appears to have done something straightaway, and to have effected something at once. For has he not made things secure for himself? And when a man has thus done something at once, he may then have a good time.

123

Ah, that is just the snare! — and that servant was cast into outer darkness. [VIII. A. 66.]

WHAT IT MEANS NOT TO TAKE RISKS

The servant in the gospel who hid his pound in the earth exemplifies this. He was wise, farsighted. Yet his master rejected him.

Imagine a case in the gospel where one of the servants came and said, " Lord, I wanted so much to gain something from the pound you entrusted to me, so I took a risk — I suppose too much of a risk, because I have gained nothing and lost my one pound." Would this man not have found forgiveness rather than that farsighted one? [X^4. A. 501.]

PRAYER

Preserve me, Lord, from the deceit of thinking that by being prudent and looking after my own interests I am necessarily using my talents aright. He who takes risks for thy sake may appear to lose, but he is accepted by thee. He who risks nothing appears to gain by his prudence, but he is rejected by thee. Let me not think that by avoiding risk I am better than the other. Grant me to see that this is an illusion. From such a snare do thou in thy mercy save me! [VIII. B. 32:3 ad.]

THE GOODLY PEARL (AND HID TREASURE)

Again, the kingdom of heaven is like unto treasure hid in a field; the which when a man hath found, he hideth, and for joy thereof goeth and selleth all that he hath, and buyeth that field. Again, the kingdom of heaven is like unto a merchantman, seeking goodly pearls: Who, when he had found one pearl of great price, went and sold all that he had, and bought it. (Matt. 13:44–46.)

The best thing in life is a find. Sometimes we seek and find; sometimes we find without having sought. He who found the pearl which he had not sought found it all the same. But if he then gives up everything in order to possess it, he expresses backward that he had already looked for it. For to *acquire* possession of a thing after having got it is just the same as looking for it.[1] [IX. A. 111; J 782.]

The man in the parable found a very costly pearl, and then went and sold all that he had and bought the same. But if he had found it, he had no need to sell anything to buy it, for it was already his.

Here we get the true Christian position. Grace cannot be bought, nor acquired. It has to be given, just as this man was given the pearl he found. He did not, that is to say, create it himself. Only then can it be bought; only then can we sell all that we have to buy it. [X². A. 50.]

Notice too that in the Scripture text above the Kingdom of Heaven is likened unto a man. One might have thought that the Kingdom of Heaven is something outside us, into which the man is received. But the Kingdom of Heaven is also "within you" (Luke 17:21), and therefore it can be likened unto a man.

Here we have the unity of the subjective and the objective. The Kingdom of Heaven, a most objective thing, is likened unto "a man," something altogether subjective. [X². A. 50 margin.]

Beautiful and uplifting it is to meet a man, whether in the pages of the gospel or in real life, who does not bargain in the market place, where the shrewdest people, calculating the odds, today buy for a high price what tomorrow the stupidest people, aided purely by chance, may buy for a low — no, he is a resolved man, who has understood what the highest good is, and moreover is

[1] What Kierkegaard means is this: The Kingdom of Heaven, which the pearl typifies, is already ours, a free gift from God. But we must discover this and enter into possession, if we are to acquire it, and this is to "*seek* the Kingdom of God." (Matt. 6:33.)

willing to pay all to buy it. It is beneficial and refreshing to see him stand there, quiet and serious, with the imperishable beauty of a resolution taken for all eternity. He has collected his possessions, he has added to them every earthly desire, everything the heart can demand, so to say, from life. He holds this before him — and then he makes his bid, not for earthly things, but for the highest good. If you see him tomorrow, unalterably he repeats his bid unaltered. If the world were to use all its cunning and all its flattery and all its terror, he still stands by his bid. All he wants is to succeed in buying the highest good.

And such a high-minded resolve is necessary if a man is to purchase the highest good. The resolve is not so much the result of long cogitations as of the deepest monition of a serious heart. [V. p. 170 f.; ED IV. p. 115 f.]

PRAYER

O Thou who givest both to begin and to end, do thou grant to the young early, when the day dawns, the resolve to will one thing — the highest good. When day declines, do thou grant to the aged an ever-fresh remembrance of that first resolve. May the last be as the first and the first as the last: the very life of him who has willed only one thing. [VIII. p. 135; PH p. 21.]

THE GREAT SUPPER

Then said he unto him, A certain man made a great supper, and bade many: and sent his servant at supper time to say to them that were bidden, Come; for all things are now ready. And they all with one consent began to make excuse. The first said unto him, I have bought a piece of ground, and I must needs go and see it: I pray thee have me excused. And another said, I have bought five yoke of oxen, and I go to prove them: I pray thee have me excused. And another said, I have married a wife, and therefore I cannot come. So that servant came, and showed his lord these things. Then the master of the house being angry said to his servant, Go out quickly into the streets and lanes of the city, and bring in hither the poor, and the maimed, and the halt, and the blind. And the servant said, Lord, it is done as thou hast commanded, and yet there is room. And the lord said unto the servant, Go out into the highways and hedges, and compel them to come in, that my house may be filled. For I say unto you, That none of those men which were bidden shall taste of my supper. (Luke 14:16–24.)

THE SERIOUS BUSINESS OF LIFE

When we hear this passage read here *in church,*[1] everyone understands it because it is easy to understand, and everyone agrees that these excuses ought not to have kept people away. But this is in God's house — in a " quiet hour," as it is called. It is there outside, where it is anything but quiet, that excuses concerning the serious business of life are made. And the only excuse for the fact that this is so is that there, outside, the highest invitation is not heard. The invitation has as it were retired from the workaday life, and sounds only in certain " quiet hours." [X³. A. 107.]

But is it not really too bad of the gospel to issue its invitation at such an inconvenient moment, just when a man is getting married, or is all engrossed in his earthly business, and so on? The invitation might better have come at a time when a man has nothing else to do, in a moment of leisure, perhaps in a " quiet hour." Really the gospel asks too much.

Yes, the gospel presents an either/or, and does it with a zeal that fairly screws us up to make a choice. However gentle the gospel is, however lovingly it invites, it never lets go this conception of itself as relentlessly presenting a choice.

One might say this is a strange kind of invitation. An ordinary invitation leaves the invited free to come or not. Yet here, when

[1] In the margin to the following little pieces, Kierkegaard writes, " I had thought of preaching on the Great Supper, and so I have given it some study." We must, therefore, especially in the first piece, imagine ourselves in church.

those invited courteously excused themselves, the Inviter sent and destroying them.[1] But this is a right which belongs to God's majesty. The wonder is, not that he destroys those who refuse him, but that he demeans himself to invite us. [X³. A. 109.]

As for ourselves, we may say that we have honestly deserved our punishment, because in our baptism we promised to accept the invitation and come. Or if that reasoning does not appeal to us, then we must say that the Inviter is God, who definitely has the right of ownership over men. [X³. A. 155.]

Notice that it was to a wedding they were invited,[2] and yet some of them excused themselves by saying they must go to a wedding. So we have two weddings. And God is so gracious as to describe his relationship to man as a love relationship. [X³. A. 107.]

PRAYER

O Thou who so early didst receive our promise, thou in whom we in baptism promised to believe — Father in heaven: grant that we may not in daily life forget this our promise, forget that we are betrothed, forget to come to thy wedding. Whatever we may find by way of excuse is of little moment. The decisive thing is that we do not come to the wedding: we who cannot excuse ourselves from accepting the invitation like those in the gospel, because we have already accepted it, and have solemnly promised to come. Therefore our guilt, if we then do not come, is only so much the greater. [X³. A. 108.]

[1] See Matt. 22:7, 13.
[2] Strictly it was not. It was to "a great supper." See Luke 14:22 ff. So Kierkegaard adds, " In the parable of the Great Supper, we are not told it was a wedding, and in the parable of the Marriage of the King's Son (Matt. 22:2 ff.) we are not told of the excuse that one had married a wife." [X³. A. 110.]

THE UNMERCIFUL SERVANT

Therefore is the kingdom of heaven likened unto a certain king, which would take account of his servants. And when he had begun to reckon, one was brought unto him, which owed him ten thousand talents. But forasmuch as he had not to pay, his lord commanded him to be sold, and his wife, and children, and all that he had, and payment to be made. The servant therefore fell down, and worshipped him, saying, Lord, have patience with me, and I will pay thee all.

Then the lord of that servant was moved with compassion, and loosed him, and forgave him the debt. But the same servant went out, and found one of his fellow servants, which owed him a hundred pence: and he laid hands on him, and took him by the throat, saying, Pay me that thou owest. . . . And his lord was wroth, and delivered him to the tormentors, till he should pay all that was due unto him. So likewise shall my heavenly Father do also unto you, if ye from your hearts forgive not every one his brother their trespasses. (Matt. 18:23–28, 34, 35.)

In the parable of the irreconcilable servant who would not forgive his fellow servant, we read, " Then he went *outside* " (v. 28). Therefore what took place between him and his lord took place *inside*. Ah! so it is with us all. *There, inwardly*, something takes place between God and us, but then when we go *outside*. . . ! [VIII. A. 76.]

It might sophistically be said of the unmerciful servant in this parable — the man to whom his lord remitted 10,000 talents while he would not even remit 100 pence to a fellow servant — " Yes, but is not the remission proportionate to the wealth of him who remits? Perhaps the 100 pence was more to the servant than the 10,000 talents to the lord. The smaller a man is, the more a little injustice injures him."

To this it must be answered that 10,000 talents is indeed a large sum to owe, but in fact each of us owes a larger. For it is sin against God that is meant in the parable; and that which sets the measure of our debts is the person to whom we owe it. [If it is God to whom I owe the debt, then the debt is great because he is great. But] I ought to regard guilt against myself as of no moment, just because I ought to judge myself of little worth. [IX. A. 491.]

The greatest expression for God's extreme severity is found in this parable, which concludes by saying that if we forgive not each other our trespasses, God will be just as severe with us as we are with others. How devastating! For we know well enough how severe we can be. But the whole point is that God is playing with us when he does toward us what we do toward others. [He could be far more severe.] [X³. A. 582.]

PRAYER

Dear God! thou hast commanded us that we must forgive our enemies; and forgive our erring brother not seven times but seventy times seven. How then couldst thou become weary of forgiving one who truly repents! [IX. A. 328.]

THE LABORERS IN THE VINEYARD

For the kingdom of heaven is like unto a man that is a householder, which went out early in the morning to hire laborers into his vineyard. And when he had agreed with the laborers for a penny a day, he sent them into his vineyard. And he went out about the third hour, and saw others standing idle in the market place, and said unto them; Go ye also into the vineyard, and whatsoever is right I will give you. And they went their way. Again he went out about the sixth and ninth hour, and did likewise. And about the eleventh hour he went out, and found others standing idle, and saith unto them, Why stand ye here all

the day idle? They say unto him, Because no man hath hired us.
He saith unto them, Go ye also into the vineyard; and whatso-
ever is right, that shall ye receive. So when even was come, the
lord of the vineyard saith unto his steward, Call the laborers,
and give them their hire, beginning from the last unto the first.
And when they came that were hired about the eleventh hour,
they received every man a penny. But when the first came, they
supposed that they should have received more; and they like-
wise received every man a penny. (Matt. 20:1–10.)

THOSE WHO ARE CALLED AT THE ELEVENTH HOUR

First Type:

We saw them as they walked so lightly on their way, so happy,
so carefree, with the buoyant spirits and high hopes of youth
upon them. Young people clung closely to them; older folk were
rejuvenated by seeing them.

Look at them now, standing there in the market place, full of
days and tired of life! It was not any rewards and honor, any
striving to win a glorious memory that had devoured their powers. No, it was the disordered enjoyment of pleasures, in whose
service they had squandered their youthful courage and all their
hope. [Yet still they are called, even at the eleventh hour.]

Second Type:

Or shall I describe for you the multitudes still in their youth
who have stood in the world without power to work or heart to
pray, shipwrecked people who had lost all, even their faith and
the confidence that it was still possible to begin to work; who
stood there, dead as an apparition amongst us? And if at times a
glint of power blazed up in their souls, then they lifted their eyes
to heaven, embittered and defiant, audaciously demanding back
from heaven what they themselves had wasted. Or if their defeat
did not express itself in such a violent outburst, perhaps a " quiet
despair" brooded over their soul. . . . But *these* also were called
at the eleventh hour. To them also sounded the earnest but gentle voice which should create hope in them.

Notice how great a difference there is between the world and Christianity. The world is not insensitive; it will give these people a tear, pity them . . . and then let them go into the paths of perdition. Not so Christianity. And if, in the blackness of despair, the divine call begat in such a person a living hope which blazed up in him with rejuvenating power, then perhaps the world might be struck by this, and could perhaps endure such a one. But if sometimes he failed; if the way proved so narrow for him that it was often characterized by backsliding, then the world would most likely denounce him. And if it has to endure hearing that they who were called at the eleventh hour are to have equal recompense with those who had borne the burden and heat of the day, then it will be *offended*.

But not so with Christians. [They must take the same " earnest but gentle " view that these might be saved even in the eleventh hour.] [II. A. 581.]

When a man comes to God, he must easily see that God has the absolute — yes, the boundlessly absolute — right to demand everything of him. But, on the other hand, the relationship is itself an absolute — yes a boundlessly absolute — depth of blessedness. But if that is so, then *eo ipso* any idea of comparison with other people is forgotten. This is clearly what the parable of the Laborers in the Vineyard teaches us. . . . Our relationship to God is obviously such a good thing, such a huge weight of blessedness, that if only I obtain it, my blessedness is, in the most absolute sense, absolute; and it is only diminished by all these worldly comparisons, which demand that my enemies shall be excluded. [VIII. A. 24; J 639.]

The reward was the same for them all, for the reward is eternal salvation, and this is something qualitative which cannot be measured in differing amounts. Those who want to have differences in the reward want to temporalize the eternal, and make it something earthly. In worldly things, the reward is quite rightly differentiated. In what is purely qualitative and eternal, the reward is all the same. In any case, if there is to be a difference, this must be fixed by the Giver himself. It cannot be demanded by the laborers. [X⁵. A. 140.]

PRAYER

Teach me, Lord, to do more than pity as the world pities. Help me to believe of all men, even those in blazing indignation against thee, or in quiet despair within themselves, that these too, even in the eleventh hour, are invited by thee unto salvation.

Teach me also to see that in comparison all is lost, love made finite, the chain of eternity broken. May I see that comparison is a selfish factor; that to love is to remain in infinite indebtedness, and that the infinity of the debt is the bond of perfection. [IX. pp. 209 f. ad; WL pp. 148 f.]

THE LOST SHEEP

What man of you, having a hundred sheep, if he lose one of them, doth not leave the ninety and nine in the wilderness, and go after that which is lost, until he find it? And when he hath found it, he layeth it on his shoulders, rejoicing. (Luke 15:4, 5.)

How it came about that the sheep got lost, we are not told. The parable begins by introducing a *lost* sheep. Yet it is clear that a sheep can be guilty for being lost, by leaving the herd. To bring about its loss, the sheep can do something itself. For its redemption, it can do nothing. [X³. A. 213.]

The shepherd takes the sheep, lays it upon his shoulders, carries it, etc. The sheep has only to be quite still. Oh, but this is only one factor! If the sheep does not die in the same moment, then it will have to struggle again in its own strength. And is it not infinitely difficult to be able to lie quite still, so that no new guilt appears; and that anxiety for the old guilt does not get the upper hand again? [X³. A. 165.]

But this is only one factor. Christianity is gentleness in severity. The severity of religion is this, that it begins by making everything more strict. It is poetical, not in the sense of being some new wishful thinking or completely new flight of fancy which poetry had not dreamed of, but as setting us difficulty; the kind of difficulty that makes men of us, just as war makes heroes. [VII. p. 434; CUP p. 398.]

Faith makes us lords, love makes us servants.[1] [X¹. A. 304.]

PRAYER

Father in heaven, let thy face shine upon me, that I may walk in thy way and not stray more distantly from thee, where thy voice can no longer reach me. Oh, let thy voice sound for me, and be heard of me, even if it overtakes me with its terrors upon my erring paths, where I live as one sick and tainted in spirit, apart and lonely, far from fellowship with thee and with men! Do thou, my Lord Jesus Christ, who came into the world to save the lost — thou who didst leave the ninety and nine sheep to seek that one which was lost — seek me, lost as I am upon my erring paths, where I am hidden from thee and from men. O thou Good Shepherd, let me hear thy gentle voice, let me know it, let me follow it! Precious Holy Spirit, come to me with groanings that cannot be uttered. (Rom. 8:26.) Pray for me as Abraham did for corrupt Sodom, that if there be but one pure thought, one better feeling in me, the time of probation may be prolonged for the barren fig tree. (Luke 13:6–9.) Precious Holy Spirit, who dost give birth to the dead and youth to the aged, renew me also; create in me a new heart. [II. A. 538.]

[1] Quoted from Luther.

THE CLEANSED LEPER: ON WITNESSING

Ye shall be witnesses unto me both in Jerusalem, and in all Judea, and in Samaria, and unto the uttermost part of the earth. (Acts 1:8.)

His leprosy was cleansed. And Jesus saith unto him, . . . Go thy way, show thyself to the priest, and offer the gift that Moses commanded, for a testimony [witness] unto them. (Matt. 8:3, 4.)

He charged them that they should tell no man: but the more he charged them, so much the more a great deal they published it. (Mark 7:36.)

The ordinary human point of view is written by human authors in their own power; and it is uncertain and wavering. The Christian point of view is written with *guided* pen; and it testifies to the Truth (this in a subjective sense) but produces nothing of its own. Hence the deep meaning which the word "witness" has in Christianity. Christians are neither the original discoverers of, nor can they improve upon, what is given. They witness, partly because Christianity is an objective act which is being realized in the world, and partly because they take this up into their own lives. [II. A. 452.]

Christ said to the leper, Show thyself to the priests *for a witness* unto them. In this last phrase there is a double meaning: " a witness unto them," because the priests must witness his cure; but also a witness to the priests that they too ought to believe in Christ. [X¹. A. 304.]

Christ forbade those he had healed to speak about their cure, but the more he forbade it, the more they did it. In Christ this was sincere, in that he did not wish for display and publicity. In the others it was sincere also, because there was danger in proclaiming the praise of Christ. Had they been cowardly and prudent, they would have said: "The Lord himself forbids it. We keep quiet because it is his will." Such collisions still happen constantly in life. It may be the duty of one side to be self-denying, of the other side to relinquish a claim. But it does not follow that it may not be paltry of the other side to take advantage of this, and say that it was the other's will. [X¹. A. 347.]

Christ left them quite free. Far from asking them to extol him, he opened out the other expedient for them, namely, that they might avoid the danger involved in extolling him and say, "He commanded us to keep silence." Precisely by their choice was it revealed what was in them. [X¹. A. 348.]

PRAYER

Grant to us, Lord, the courage to bear witness to thee, and to show forth thy praise both with our lips and with our lives. May the light of our Christian faith so shine before men that they may see the light, and glorify thee, O our Father, who art in heaven.[1]

THE TEN LEPERS

And as he entered into a certain village, there met him ten men that were lepers, which stood afar off: and they lifted up their voices, and said, Jesus, Master, have mercy on us. And when he saw them, he said unto them, Go show yourselves unto the priests. And it came to pass, that, as they went, they were cleansed. And one of them, when he saw that he was healed, turned back, and with a loud voice glorified God, and fell down on his face at his feet, giving him thanks: and he was a Samaritan. And Jesus answering said, Were there not ten cleansed? but where are the nine? There are not found that returned to give glory to God, save this stranger. And he said unto him, Arise, go thy way: thy faith hath made thee whole. (Luke 17:12–19.)

[1] Adapted from the above.

(a) Notice how the nine were healed of their leprosy — and then brought upon themselves a still worse leprosy by their ingratitude and discourtesy.

(b) Notice the difference between the sickness of the body and the sickness of the soul. Sickness of the body is known of itself. The leper did not need to draw attention to the fact that he was sick. He only had to call upon Christ to heal him.

(c) That ingratitude was a sickness did not occur to these lepers at all; which only raised their ingratitude to a new potency. They did not see that they needed Christ for the sickness of ingratitude.

(d) The perilous fact about spiritual sickness is that one must already be in possession of a certain amount of health before one notices and recognizes and confesses that one is sick. [X². A. 103.]

It is usual, in explaining this miracle, to omit what is Christianly so important, namely the situation it created. We stress the ingratitude of the lepers, and overlook the important point that by thanking Christ the lepers would lay themselves out to suffer hatred for his sake. We forget that the priests, to whom these men were to show themselves in obedience to Christ, would naturally do all they could to prevent the lepers from being grateful to him.

Indeed I am almost tempted to regard it as a trial put upon these men by Christ, when he told them to go and show themselves to the priests. For he knew well enough that the priests would say all they could to prevent them from being grateful to him. They would represent gratitude as being a crime against God — blasphemy, in fact. [X². A. 206.]

PRAYER

O Lord our God! To thee we cry in the hour of need, thee we thank in the hour of joy. Oh, beautiful it is to thank when one can readily understand that thou art giving good and perfect gifts; when even the fleshly heart is ready and eager to understand and even the earthly understanding hastens to agree! Yet more blessed still it is to thank thee when life is a dark speech; more blessed to thank thee when the heart is oppressed, when the mind is darkened, when the understanding becomes treacherous by reason of ambiguity, and the memory deceitful through forget-fulness, when self-love, terrified, shudders back, when prudence opposes, if not in defiance, at any rate in despondency — more blessed then to thank God. For he who thus thanks loves God. He dares to say to thee, thou Omniscient One, "Lord thou knowest all things, thou knowest that I love thee." [VII. A. 132.]

A MAN SICK OF THE PALSY:
THE EXCUSING HEART

And, behold, they brought to him a man sick of the palsy, ly-ing on a bed: and Jesus seeing their faith said unto the sick of the palsy; Son, be of good cheer; thy sins be forgiven thee. And, behold, certain of the scribes said within themselves, This man blasphemeth. (Matt. 9:2, 3.)

Ye are they which justify yourselves before men; but God knoweth your hearts. (Luke 16:15.)

The scribes were outwardly holy, but inwardly sinful. Jesus saw through the outer mask, as he always does; and it behooves us to ask, Are our *hearts* free from the thralldom of sin, however seemly our outward life may be? For our hearts often pay far greater toll to sin than do our words or deeds. They invite us to self-excusing. More often in thought than in word or deed do we excuse ourselves by saying, "I could not help it: it is my nature." Thoughts invite us, more than words and deeds, to continue in sin; for thought can be concealed, while words and deeds can-not. Thoughts also, far more than words or deeds, prevent repentance, because they cut away the punishment and suffering and humility which we are called of God to suffer here in this world.[1] [II. A. 13.]

Do we perhaps forget, when speaking or thinking, that God in heaven is not checked by any illusion, that his thought is vivid and present, that it pierces through everything, and judges the designs of the heart? [III. p. 315; ED I. p. 75.]

PRAYER

I seek thee, thou the Omniscient. If I am guilty, enlighten my understanding that I may see my error and my depravity. I do not wish to escape suffering—that is not my prayer—but let me learn never to argue with thee. I must conquer, even though the manner of it is infinitely different from what I can imagine. [VI. p. 245; S p. 219 f.]

PALSY: GOOD CHEER

And, behold, they brought to him a man sick of the palsy, lying on a bed: and Jesus seeing their faith said unto the sick of the palsy; Son, be of good cheer; thy sins be forgiven thee. And, behold, certain of the scribes said within themselves, This man blasphemeth. And Jesus knowing their thoughts said, Wherefore think ye evil in your hearts? (Matt. 9:2–4.)

Spiritually understood, it is always the case that the man who thinks he must steer his own life and do all his own calculating and so on is sick of the palsy. How he drags on, year after year it may be, tormented by all his calculations! He drags on like a paralytic till faith comes with the words, " Rise up and walk."

[1] This was a rough note for a sermon; I have slightly filled it out.

And note the words, " Take thy bed," and walk. This shows how strong he is now to become, for the bed which formerly carried him he now himself carries. He is so strong that he no longer needs artificial support of that kind. [X³. A. 537.]

CHRISTIAN " GOOD CHEER "

" My son be of good cheer, thy sins are forgiven thee." The " good cheer " of being forgiven means:

1. *Freedom.* Yet not a freedom that is outside the ambit of the law. It is not freedom to do as we like. The Commandments must still be obeyed — thou shalt not kill, thou shalt not commit adultery, etc.

2. The " good cheer " of forgiveness is hope fulfilled *now*. Otherwise, hope is like an old lady who only stares longingly at the future, and has no satisfaction in the present.

3. The " good cheer " of forgiveness leads to power and action. Hebrews 3:6 tells us to " hold fast our boldness and the glorying of our hope firm to the end." The " glorying " expresses, as it were, our boldness because of our " good cheer."

Distinguish (*a*) good cheer before men (*b*) good cheer before God. To illustrate the latter, let me take a picture. Sometimes our physical eye turns toward heaven. We are overwhelmed by the infinite distance, and our eye finds no resting place between heaven and earth. But when the eye of the soul seeks God, and we again feel the infinite distance, then it is that the " good cheer " of forgiveness comes in, to bridge, as it were, the distance. For in this case we have a Mediator between God and man, even Christ who gives us the " good cheer " of forgiveness.[1] [II. A. 326.]

" WHY THINK YE EVIL IN YOUR HEARTS? "

The question applies to the whole of the Pharisees' life, with their outward holiness but inward hypocrisy.

But, you may ask, are not our thoughts our own? Are they not tax-free, so to say? No; on the contrary, they pay far greater toll

[1] Slightly expanded.

to sin than do words or deeds. For instance they invite us to excuse ourselves. I could not help it; it is my nature, we let ourselves think. But we cannot get away with this quite so easily in word or in deed as we do in thought. Men do not excuse us as easily as we excuse ourselves.

And so our thoughts inveigle us to continue as we are. For they can be concealed; whereas words and deeds cannot.

And, once more, thoughts may prevent conversion. For they would persuade us to avoid all the punishment and suffering and humility in this world to which we are called of God. How can we be converted if we try to cut such things out? [1] [II. A. 13.]

PRAYER

" Let not your heart be troubled, neither let it be afraid." (John 14:27.) O God, help us to see that we have cause to be troubled and afraid when the world gives. Save us from " shrinking back into perdition " (Heb. 10:39), and give us " faith unto the saving of our souls." [IX. A. 355 ad.]

THE FEEDING OF THE FIVE THOUSAND: " SEEK YE FIRST THE KINGDOM OF HEAVEN "

In those days the multitude being very great, and having nothing to eat, Jesus called his disciples unto him, and saith unto them, I have compassion on the multitude, because they have now been with me three days, and have nothing to eat: and if I send them away fasting to their own houses, they will faint by the way: for divers of them came from far. And his disciples answered him, From whence can a man satisfy these men with bread here in the wilderness? And he asked them, How many

[1] Rough notes designed for a sermon, which therefore I have ventured to expand.

loaves have ye? And they said, Seven. And he commanded the people to sit down on the ground: and he took the seven loaves, and gave thanks, and brake, and gave to his disciples to set before them; and they did set them before the people. And they had a few small fishes: and he blessed, and commanded to set them also before them. So they did eat, and were filled: and they took up of the broken meat that was left seven baskets. And they that had eaten were about four thousand: and he sent them away. (Mark 8:1–9.)

From life's manifold activities Christ called the people to him. He spoke to them of heavenly things. He once dismissed those who sought earthly things, and said, " Let the dead bury their dead." He moved among men as a shining example of how little a man needs. He had not where to lay his head. His meat was to do his Father's will. But if he had then left the earth; if after having taught men, he had dismissed them and said: " Go away and feed yourselves, I know nothing of these cares, and I scorn them " . . . But he did not. He had compassion on the multitude. He knew men's needs because he had *hungered in the wilderness.* He did not put asunder what God had joined together, but invited them when he said, " Seek ye first the Kingdom of God and all these things shall be added unto you."

So it was here. They had followed Christ to be taught, and to learn how to find God's Kingdom. They did not ask for food, but it was *added* unto them.

Consider God's care. If we are content with simple things, we shall generally find we have enough. But we must lift our minds to higher things. Later Christ blamed these very people. They came, he said, not because they saw his signs and miracles, but because they ate and were filled. God's care for earthly things should make us think of higher things, not make us more unreasonable in our wishes. [III. A. 87.]

PRAYER

O Lord our God, all creation looks up to thee, and expects food and drink from thee. Thou dost uplift thy gentle hand and fill all things living with blessing. Thou hearest the cry of the beast, thou heedest the complaint of man. They lift their thoughts to thee: those to whom thou hast given much, because they know that everything comes from thee, and that no abundance satisfies unless thou dost bless it; those to whom thou hast given little, because they know that no gift from thee is so small but that by thy blessing it may become an abundance. [III. A. 86.]

CANA: A WEDDING AND A WOMAN

And the third day there was a marriage in Cana of Galilee; and the mother of Jesus was there: and both Jesus was called, and his disciples, to the marriage. Jesus saith unto her, Woman, what have I to do with thee? mine hour is not yet come. Jesus saith unto them, Fill the waterpots with water. And they filled them up to the brim. And he saith unto them, Draw out now, and bear unto the governor of the feast. And they bare it. When the ruler of the feast had tasted the water that was made wine, and knew not whence it was, (but the servants which drew the water knew,) the governor of the feast called the bridegroom, and saith unto him, Every man at the beginning doth set forth good wine; and when men have well drunk, then that which is worse: but thou hast kept the good wine until now. (John 2:1, 2, 4, 7–10.)

In the life of every Christian the same miracle is repeated that surprised those present at the marriage in Cana. "Thou hast poured out the poor wine first, and then the good." What I have said will be accepted by all who have experienced how the world first pours out the good wine and then the bad. [II. A. 317; J 246.]

Each miracle of truth is like the miracle at Cana. Truth pours out the poor wine first, and keeps the best till last. The deceitful world, on the contrary, pours out its best wine first. [V. p. 96; ED IV. p. 20.]

The gospel story of the marriage in Cana might be thus explained: it was the *first* miracle because it stands like a motto over the whole of Christ's life — first suffering, then glorification.[1]

Observe also that Christ's words to Mary, "Woman, what have I to do with thee?" have a certain faint resemblance to the words he once spoke to Peter: "Get thee behind me Satan, thou art an offense unto me." I mean that there is here in Mary (as there was in Peter) something of that human impatience which wants help immediately. [X². A. 85; J 977.]

PRAYER

Father in heaven, teach us to walk before thy face, and let not our thoughts and deeds, like strangers who come from afar, pay a passing visit to thy dwelling places. Rather let us, like those who dwell at home, feel that thou art amongst us. For what doth it avail us if such a visit be never so glorious; what avails it if our face shine like Moses' face when he talked with God; what avails it though we hide our faces (as Moses hid his from the Israelites) in order not to notice how quickly the splendor vanishes? Let us never forget, Lord, that all Christianity is a *pilgrimage,* and that though I stand at the uttermost edge of the Kingdom, holy Father, far away and alone like the publican of old, yet if I only stand with my face *toward* thee, and do not, like the man who put his hand to the plow, turn myself away; if I only stand with staff in hand, ready for the journey, albeit mountains and dales and raging torrents lie before me, yet have I still thy promise that the least in the Kingdom of Heaven is greater than any born of woman. [II. A. 377.]

[1] I.e., the "bad wine" — the cup of suffering — must be drunk before the "good wine" — the cup of glory — can be drunk.

PART
V

GENERAL

THE FATHERHOOD OF GOD —
I: ITS STRENGTH

For this cause I bow my knees unto the Father of our Lord Jesus Christ, of whom the whole family in heaven and earth is named, that he would grant you, according to the riches of his glory, to be strengthened with might by his Spirit in the inner man. (Eph. 3:14–16.)

Good fortune and evil fortune alike serve to strengthen us with might in the inward man. But no man can give this strengthening to himself; and he who receives a testimony is not the one who gives it. The testimony itself is a gift from God, from whom all good gifts come, the most glorious of all, a gift from our Father in heaven, of whom all fatherhood is named, in heaven and on earth.

He who looks only upon the external — to him the expression " God the Father " is figurative and unreal. For if he thinks, God gives the good gifts as a father does — which, as it were, proves that God is our Father — then he is judging externally, and the truth itself becomes for him but figurative.

But the inward man looks not upon the gifts but upon the Giver. Joy and sorrow, fortune and misfortune, need and victory, are to him all alike gifts, because the Giver is his chief concern. The inward man knows and is convinced that God is a Father in heaven, and that in saying this he is not using a mere common or loose phrase but the most proper and true expression possible. For God not only gives the gifts, but gives himself with the gifts. That is a thing human beings cannot do. They can be present *with* the gift only in a feeling or word; they cannot saturate the whole content of the gift down to the least particle with this feeling.

It is not because you have a father, or because people in general have fathers, that God is called Father in heaven. Rather, it is after him that all fatherhood in heaven and earth is named. And even if you had the best father there is among men, yet he was only a foster father compared with the fatherhood from which all fatherhood in heaven or earth is named. [III. pp. 347 f.; ED I. p. 116.]

Only the inward man recognizes that God is Father; for the inward man asks not about the gift but the Giver. [IV. B. 158. § 6 and 7.]

Misfortune may come from other people, but God allows it. Or it can come from God, and then it is God's testing. [IV. B. 151. § 3.]

Every piece of evidence which comes from God is a strengthening in the inward man. This is true also of happiness, good fortune, or joy. He who builds his barns the greater and thanks God, is not this a strengthening? [IV. B. 151. § 7.]

PRAYER

Give what thou wilt — but give only the testimony with thy gift, and therein thyself. If thou givest joy, may I be glad in thee. If care, then may I cast care upon thee. May I receive all thou dost send, so only I retain the testimony: yea, even the summons of death itself, so only it come with greetings and testimony from thee. Let not joys separate us from thee in the forgetfulness of pleasure; nor sorrow set a barrier between thee and us. Amen. [IV. B. 151. § 1.]

THE FATHERHOOD OF GOD —
II: ITS UNIVERSALITY

For this cause I bow my knees unto the Father of our Lord Jesus Christ, of whom the whole family in heaven and earth is named, that he would grant you, according to the riches of his glory, to be strengthened with might by his Spirit in the inner man. (Eph. 3:14–16.)

Does it seem to you that when your thought goes out from your paternal home and waywardly fares forth into the wide world in order to rise to the conception of God as the almighty Creator of all things and yet also the common Father of all — does it seem that you miss something of the kind of love you shared in your paternal home, where your earthly father was *your* father only, and you alone his child? And in consequence does it seem to you that the picture of God as the general Father will not quite do? You feel then that such earthly conceptions ought not to be used — and I too admit that the picture does not quite fit the facts.

But when you were anxious and worried, and came to your earthly father to find comfort and peace, perhaps you found him also bowed down with grief; so that his sorrow did not alleviate your own, but only increased it. If only for a moment, you forgot your own sufferings out of sympathy for his. But when on the other hand you were torn asunder and weak, and turned your heart and mind to Him who cares for all, and found him always a strength to the weak one — yes, and the more of a strength the weaker you became — even then, my friend, the picture will not quite do. And well it is for you, the more you perceive that the picture will not quite do. Aforetime you perceived with a certain sorrow that although you had taken the best thing you had upon earth in order to describe what belonged to heaven, it did not get you there, but melted and disappeared on the way. This, however, is not the case now; because now you have perceived that God is not called Father after an earthly designation. On the contrary, it is (as the Scripture says) after him, your Heavenly Father, that all fatherhood has its name in heaven and on earth. The name "father" does not struggle upward from earth to heaven, but descends from heaven to earth. Even if you have the best father there is upon earth, he is still only your foster father; only a weak reflection of the fatherhood after which your earthly father is named; only a shadow, a reflection, a picture, and analogy, a "dark speech" about the Fatherhood from which all fatherhood in heaven and earth is named. [III. C. 12.]

PRAYER

Thou hast all good gifts, and thy bounty is greater than human understanding can grasp. Thou art willing to give, and thy goodness is greater than human understanding can grasp. Yet no man dare ask it of thee. We ask thee, and this is our comfort, because thou dost fulfill every prayer; for either thou dost give what we pray for, or something far better than what we pray for. [IV. B. 151.]

JOY — COURAGE

While they yet believed not for joy. (Luke 24:41.)

When she knew Peter's voice, she opened not the gate for gladness. (Acts 12:14.)

There is something joyful in the very fact that "for joy" we scarcely dare believe what is so exceedingly glorious.

You do not believe it? But take courage, for after all it is really only because it is all too glorious. Take courage, for it is joy that is hindering you. Is not this itself a joyful thing? [VIII. A. 300.]

"Ask and ye shall receive, that your joy may be full." (John 16:24.) Thus Christianity would teach us that prayer, blessed as it is in itself, reaches toward something more blessed, and is not itself the height of blessedness. In comparison to earthly things, prayer is indeed greater than mundane blessings. But the blessedness of heaven is something greater even than prayer. [VIII. A. 532.]

That you can at any moment shut your door and speak with God, without any person between, without any of the strain and weight we feel when a person of distinction condescends to us — is not this glorious? But you do not believe it? That is because it is all too joyful. And is not this in itself a joyful thing?

The same is true of the forgiveness of sins. [VIII. A. 302.]

That which would frighten us away from God — may not this be the very thing to lead us nearer to him? Sin would frighten us away — but in reconciliation, it is precisely our consciousness of sin that leads us nearer to God. For there is hope of conquering the evil, if only, every time it attacks us, it leads us nearer to God. [VIII. A. 284.]

There is something joyful in the fact that the more the world goes against us, the less we are retarded on the way in our journey to heaven. In other words, misfortune, Christianly understood, is good fortune. Everything that helps us on the way we should go is indeed to be regarded as good fortune. But this is precisely what misfortune does. Therefore it is good fortune. [VIII. A. 322.]

It is the genesis of hope. [VIII. A. 361.]

There is a hope that is but a playfellow of childhod. It is not steadfast in trials. There is another hope that is recruited in trial ("experience worketh hope" — Rom. 5:4). This is steadfast, and

" maketh not ashamed " (Rom. 5:5). It is strongest when suffering is greatest. [IV. B. 151. § 3.]

PRAYER

Lord Jesus! When I am tempted to doubt whether my sins are forgiven me, may I find assurance in hearing thee as it were say to me: " Believe it nevertheless. I have given my life to win for thee the forgiveness of sins." And may I then believe it, for no greater guarantee is possible. [XII. p. 306 ad; TC pp. 270 f.]

" COME UNTO ME "

Come unto me, all ye that labor and are heavy laden, and I will give you rest. (Matt. 11:28.)

When a true and faithful friend says to one of us: " You seem, dear one, to be unhappy. Come to me; perhaps my company will comfort you," would you not then with thankfulness accept his invitation? Would you not also have his loving invitation in thankful remembrance when he had completed his course here upon earth, and only consorted with you in the lightning flashes of thought? But there may also occur moments in which he did not come to you with his usual friendliness, perhaps through being out of tune or weighed down — moments in which he seemed almost lost to you. Nevertheless you have felt the sacredness of some moments and you know what they mean. Why then do you hesitate to follow a voice that is not in the least strange to you, but, on the contrary, has been familiar since your earliest days, and has sounded in your ears from your childhood; a voice that says just as mildly, just as tenderly, just as freely as any friend, " Come unto me, all ye that suffer and are heavy laden "? Arms are open for you in which you can rest just as securely, just as sweetly, as in the arms of your best friend, although *these* arms embrace " all those who suffer and are heavy laden " — embrace them all with equal tenderness; for it was only in our Saviour's earthly life that John alone lay upon his bosom. " Come hither; oh, come hither! " Thus may the minister of the gospel also call. But is this voice of his then a voice which prepares the way of the Lord only in the wilderness? Does it not concern us also, who, by our upbringing, family life, and whole development, are brought very closely in touch with Christianity? Yes, indeed; to us also it sounds as a beckoning voice, which every moment is prepared to comfort us, every moment prepared to lead us forward. " Come hither; oh, come hither! " until at last it lays aside all the sorrowfulness which has characterized it and sounds like an angel song, like familiar music for all who have listened to it, saying with eternal love, " Come hither ye blessed of my Father, inherit the Kingdom prepared for you from the beginning of the world." [II. A. 761.]

PRAYER

Thou who madest the great surrender dost here surrender thyself anew. It is thou thyself who seekest those who stand in need of help, thou who alone canst help, and help with the one thing needful. For thou savest from the only sickness that, in the truest sense, is deadly.

Yet thou dost not wait for us to come to thee. Thou dost come of thine own accord to us, uncalled for. It is thou who dost call us, and offer us thy help — and what help! Oh, wonderful is thy love; wonderful that thou who hast help to give art the one who says, " Come hither "! [XII. pp. 24. 23 ad; TC pp. 11. 10.]

IN CHURCH

I was glad when they said unto me, Let us go into the house of the Lord. (Ps. 122:1.)

REFLECTION BEFORE A CHURCH SERVICE

We shall not necessarily reflect upon, or get to know, anything we did not know before, but we shall meditate. And by God's help we shall have something to meditate upon. [X¹. A. 211.]

REFLECTION AFTER THE SERVICE

If you have not felt that God is present here, and that you are before him, then your visit to God's house has been in vain. For all else that you have seen and heard has been of no consequence, and you might just as well have remained at home. . . . On the other hand, if at home you could feel quite vividly that God is present, and that you are before him, then you could in another sense properly have remained at home. For certainly this place is God's house, but the point is that your own house should become a house of God. And certainly this place is a holy place, but the point is that your drawing room also ought to be a holy place. And with regard to what is sacred, the position is not so much that you shall go forth to it, but that you should take it home to yourself. It may rightly be, with regard to pleasure and relaxation, that you go forth for it; and it may not be good that you should have it at home with you. But with regard to what is divine, you must not go forth for it so much. And in any case, every time you do, you must strive to take it home with you. [X¹. A. 212.]

PRAYER

Thou All-present! When the preacher considered how he would speak and what he would say, then thou wert present. When any individual decided to go up to thine house, and went, thou wert present. But perhaps this fact was not very vivid to him. Bless thou then our service, that we all, every one of us, especially at this hour, may feel thy presence, and that we are before thee. [X¹. A. 210.]

UNCONDITIONAL SURRENDER
AN ABSOLUTE DEMAND

And it came to pass, that, as they went in the way, a certain man said unto him, Lord, I will follow thee whithersoever thou goest. And Jesus said unto him, Foxes have holes, and birds of the air have nests; but the Son of man hath not where to lay his head. And he said unto another, Follow me. But he said, Lord, suffer me first to go and bury my father. Jesus said unto him, Let the dead bury their dead: but go thou and preach the kingdom of God. And another also said, Lord, I will follow thee; but let me first go bid them farewell, which are at home at my house. And Jesus said unto him, No man, having put his hand to the plow, and looking back, is fit for the kingdom of God. (Luke 9:57–62.)

You must give yourself to Christ unconditionally. Nothing, nothing, be it the greatest triviality or something tremendously important in your eyes, must be so put between yourself and him that it becomes a condition, and means that in such a case you cannot surrender yourself. No, the surrender must be unconditional. Then — and this is a different thing from making prior conditions — you can pray for yourself that your burden may not be too heavy.

The defect in the man in the gospel who wanted to be a disciple, but must first bury his father, is that he wanted this *first*. He made this a condition; and if this condition were not granted to him, he would not surrender. In other words he would only surrender himself conditionally. He ought to have yielded unconditionally and said to Jesus: "Even if it is demanded of me that I should let go that which I so eagerly wanted, namely to bury my father — then I do let it go. I give myself unconditionally. This about burying my father is not a condition I make beforehand. No, it is a prayer I make to thee *after* I have surrendered myself, asking humbly whether it may not be granted."

It is certainly true that by this unconditional giving of yourself to Christ, who is Absolute Spirit and death from the world, you run the risk that he may make things awkward for you — so awkward that you feel almost ready to despair. This is, and must be, the thing about unconditional surrender that makes flesh and blood tremble. So it must be. But remember also that Christ is grace, and it is to grace that you surrender. [X³. A. 393.]

THE ABSOLUTENESS OF CHRISTIANITY

A man comes to Christ and wants to be his disciple; he only asks that Christ will wait a few days while he buries his deceased father. Then he will forsake all and follow Him. Christ answers: "Let the dead bury their dead. Come thou and follow me." (Matt. 8:22.) God in heaven! See what a proof is here, that Christ has an absolute conception that his cause is the absolute. For he demands that we should take up his standard and break with everything else. Truly never man spoke in this fashion. It is true enough that the better anyone's cause is, the more severe he is in choosing his disciples. But next after this absolute break, can anything be imagined more beautiful than the stipulation that only a few days' grace be granted in which to bury a deceased father! No human being whatsoever has had a cause so absolute that it could induce him to refuse such a disciple. Nay, a mere man would rather commend the filial piety which the disciple here displays. But Christ and Christ alone *had* such an absolute cause.

And what exaltation, which again can only be divine, quietly to repose in the consciousness of the absoluteness of his cause, and refuse such a disciple! Never has any man serving a cause had also, with the cause, this absolute independence, not needing help from any other person. This is again the absoluteness of divinity.

But it is clear that such a cause as Christ had is unique. It was a cause which, unlike other causes, did not need support to enable it to conquer. No, Christ's business was precisely to take care that eventually he did *not* " conquer " (though conquer he easily could). Hence there was certainly a reason for being strict. Otherwise Christ might get disciples who would help him to conquer; whereas his business was to arrange everything so that he should die.

O wonderful cause! Yet here again the Absolute is expressed, which is divine. No man has ever had a cause in the same sense as Christ. Many a man has lost a cause, but never has any man had a cause whose very nature it was that it should be lost, so that he must actually work for such a loss. This again shows the superhuman element in Christ's cause, which is altogether heterogeneous from everything human. It is related only to itself. It does not come into the world in order to get its fate decided; but, eternally decided in itself as to what it wants, it comes into the world — to be slain. [X³. A. 193.]

When a person only has contact with God, then the relationship is as a child to a father.

When Christ comes in as well, then the person is treated as a grownup. Imitation and the exercise of free will [are now demanded. These] show that now a higher demand is being made than to a child.

Yet it must also be emphatically remembered that Christ is Grace as well; and that he himself is the one who helps us to strive. [X. A. 378.]

PRAYER

Father in heaven, grant that nothing, no " first," may come between me and thee. Enable me to surrender to thee unconditionally; and then do thou listen to my heart's deepest desires. And if thy demands be hard, may I know that Christ is grace, and that his unconditional demands, made by him severely, yet calmly and independently, are made because his cause is self-determined — a cause which, though it seemed lost in his death, is thereby won.[1]

FAITH AWAITS NOT PROOFS, BUT VENTURES

God was manifest in the flesh, justified in the Spirit, seen of angels, preached unto the Gentiles, believed on in the world, received up into glory. (I Tim. 3:16.)

All the factors here enumerated, except one, are of a purely historical kind, and are told in the same way as other historical events: e.g., manifested in the flesh, seen of angels, preached unto the Gentiles, received up into glory. But the words " believed on in the world " — do they also merely make a historical statement, and merely give a piece of news which you know from the mouth of others? Or do they mean something far deeper? Are you and your life able to bear witness to yourself and others about the truth of the words, " He was believed on in the world "?

If the firmness of your conviction about these words is more or less dependent on what others say, then remember that after the words " believed on in the world " follows the phrase, " He was received up in glory." Our earthly existence was given as a period for our repentance.[2] . . .

" Preached unto the Gentiles." True, many nations do not come to Christ in this world. But you cannot fob off things by this. Was he not offered for you? Do you know the ways of Providence? Were you not among the many called? Or will you soothe yourself by thinking that many are in a like case with you? Would you

<hr>

[1] Adapted from the above.   [2] Cf. Acts 5:31.

fob off your sorrow for a father's death by the thought that 100,-000 die daily on earth? You must not so tempt God. [II. A. 1.]

Everybody living in Christendom has enough information about Christianity to be able to invoke Christ — to supplicate him and prayerfully to turn to him. If a man does that with a deep sense of need, and in honesty of heart, he will certainly become a believer. If only it is quite certain before God that this man feels the desire to believe, he will quite certainly get to know what he is to believe. The opposite is, without desire to believe, to inquire, ponder, meditate, waste year after year of his life in trifles, and at last lose his blessedness too, through trying to get quite literally definite, even to the very dot, what he has to believe. This " opposite " is a hollow sham. [X. p. 284; CD p. 250.]

PRAYER

Lord, may these my quiet times of meditation with thee, help me to say with increasing reality, " He was believed on in the world." [II. A. 1 ad.]

" Lord I believe, help thou mine unbelief." [Mark 9:24.]

SIN — DESPAIR

And I say unto you my friends, Be not afraid of them that kill the body, and after that have no more that they can do. But I will forewarn you whom ye shall fear: Fear him, which after he hath killed hath power to cast into hell; yea, I say unto you, Fear him. (Luke 12:4, 5.)

" Fear not them who only can kill the body." Physically it is indeed true that a man can fall by the hand of another. Spiritually the truth is that a man can fall only by his own hand. No one can corrupt him except himself.

Evil does not destroy the soul in the same way that sickness

destroys the body. The body at last gives out, or it dies of sickness. But the soul continues to be. It is, as is well known, upon
this that Socrates based a proof for the immortality of the soul.[1]
[VII. A. 206.]

Sin is man's destruction. Only the rust of sin can destroy the
soul — or rather *eternally* destroy it. Sin is not just a thoroughfare
which all have to go through sometime. Rather, it is something
from which we must all flee. Sin is not the affair of a moment. It
is an eternal fall from the eternal. It is not therefore a thing of
" one time," nor can its " one time " become " no time." [2] [X. p.
125; CD p. 108.]

When death is the greatest danger, one hopes for life. But
when one becomes acquainted with an even more dreadful danger, one hopes for death. And when the danger is so great that
death has become hope, then despair is the despondency of not
being able even to die.

In this last sense despair is sickness unto death. It is this ago-
nizing contradiction, this sickness in the self, eternally to die, to
die and yet not to die, to " die the death." For " to die " means
that all is over. But " to die the death " means to experience death
while living. And if this can be done for one single moment, it
means that it can be done for all eternity. If a man were to die of
despair as one dies of sickness, then the eternal part of him, the
self, could die in the same way as the body dies of sickness. But
this is impossible. . . . Socrates proved the immortality of the
soul from the fact that the sickness of the soul (sin) does not consume it as bodily sickness consumes the body. Similarly one could
prove the eternal in man from the fact that despair does not consume his self, and that this fact is precisely the torment of contradiction in despair. If there were nothing eternal in man, he
could not despair. And if despair could consume his soul, still despair would not exist. [XI. p. 151; SD p. 30.]

[1] Cf. Plato's *Republic* 608D–611A.
[2] By the last phrase Kierkegaard means that you cannot just delete
sin as if it had not been. Its corrupting effect is deeper and more per-
manent than that.

PRAYER

Father in heaven! Go with us as formerly thou didst go with
the Jews of old time. O let us not think we have grown away from
thy upbringing, but let us grow into it, grow under it, as the
good seed grows in patience. Let us not forget what thou hast
done for us, and if thy help has been wonderfully forthcoming,
let us not, like ungrateful creatures, seek it again because we ate
and were filled. Let us feel that without thee we can do nothing,
but let us not feel this in craven weakness but in strong assurance,
having the joyful conviction that thou art with the weak. [II. A.
327.]

CHOICE

*I call heaven and earth to record this day against you, that I
have set before you life and death, blessing and cursing: therefore choose life, that both thou and thy seed may live. (Deut.
30:19.)*

A choice! Do you, my hearer, know how in a single word to express anything that is more glorious? Do you know, even if you
were to talk year in and year out, how you could mention anything more glorious than a choice, to possess the power of choice?
For though no doubt it is true that the only blessed thing is to
choose aright, yet the faculty of choice itself is truly the glorious
prerequisite. What does it matter to the maiden to take note of
all the outstanding qualities of her future lord if she herself cannot choose? And, on the other hand, what more glorious thing
does she know how to say than when, whether others praise the
beloved's many perfections or mention his many faults, she says,
" He is my heart's choice! "? A choice! Yes, this is the jewel of
great price, yet not intended to be buried and hidden away; for

a choice that is not used is worse than nothing; it is a snare in which a man entangled himself as a slave, who did not become free — by choosing. It is a good thing which you never can be rid of. It remains with you, and, if you do not use it, it becomes a curse. A choice — not between red and green, not between silver and gold — no, a choice between God and the world! Do you know anything greater to set beside choice? Do you know any more overwhelming and humbling expression for God's condescension and indulgence toward man than that he places Himself, so to say, on the same level of choice with the world, yet only in order that man may be able to choose; that God, if language dare speak thus, woos mankind — that he, the eternal Might, woos feeble mankind because in fact the strong always does woo the weaker? Yet, how insignificant is the maiden's choice between her lovers by comparison with this choice between God and the world! A choice! Or is it perhaps an imperfection in the choice that is here discussed, that man not only can choose, but that he *must* choose? Would it not, then, be very profitable for a young maiden if she had a serious-minded father who said to her, " My dear girl, you have your freedom; you may choose for yourself, but you *must* choose." Or would it be more useful to her that she had the choice but coquettishly chose and chose again, and never reached making a choice?

No, man *must* choose; for so does God retain His honor, while at the same time having a fatherly concern for man. Though God has condescended to be that which *can be chosen,* yet man *must* on his part, choose. God does not allow himself to be mocked. Therefore the matter stands thus: If a man neglects to choose, then that is the same as the presumption of choosing the world.

Man must choose between God and mammon. This is the eternal, unchangeable condition of choice, which can never be evaded — no, not to all eternity. None shall be able to say: " God and mammon, they are not, after all, so absolutely different. One can combine them both in the choice," for this is to refrain from choosing. When there is a choice between two, then to want to choose both is just to " shrink, to one's own perdition " (Heb.

10:39) from the choice. None shall be able to say, "One can choose a little of mammon, and also God as well." No, oh, no, it is presumptuous mockery of God if anybody thinks that only he who desires great wealth chooses mammon. Alas! he who craves for a farthing, without God, wants to have a farthing for himself. He chooses mammon. A farthing is enough, the choice is made, he has chosen mammon; that it is little makes not the slightest difference. . . . God is present in the moment of choice, not as a witness of it, but that He may be chosen. And God's being present in order that he may be chosen is that which gives eternal significance to the decision of the choice. But that way of speaking which would forbid God, because he is so exalted, from allowing himself to be chosen, is mockery of God. To set a crown of thorns upon God's head, and spit upon him, is mockery of God; but to make God so exalted that his presence becomes mere imagination, becomes of no account — that is also mockery of God.

And so man has to choose. Terrible is the battle, the battle in man's inmost being, between God and the world. The crowning risk involved lies in the possession of choice. But what, then, is the blessedness that is promised when the choice is made aright; or, which is the same thing, what must man choose? He must choose God's Kingdom and his righteousness. For this he is to give up all, quite indifferently of whether this all be millions or a single penny. Only when a man, though he toil and spin, is yet like the lily which does not toil and spin; only when a man, though he sow and reap and gather into barns, is quite like the bird which does not sow, and does not reap, and does not gather into barns — only then does he not serve mammon. [VIII. pp. 341 ff.; CL pp. 64 ff.]

PRAYER

O God, teach me so deeply to understand myself that I may understand how utterly impossible it is to be satisfied with the mere fact that I am the master of my own destiny; and that there is no satisfaction and joy and bliss for a man except in obedience. [VIII. A. 525 ad.]

THE CHRIST WHO COMES

Behold, I stand at the door, and knock: if any man hear my voice, and open the door, I will come in to him, and will sup with him, and he with me. (Rev. 3:20.)

Surely I come quickly: Amen. Even so, come, Lord Jesus. (Rev. 22:20.)

We read that Christ after his resurrection came through closed doors, where the disciples were assembled. This is sometimes mistakenly used as a picture of how eagerly Christ seeks the soul, how he can even get through the closed doors of hearts that are indifferent or hardened. But this is untrue.[1] Rather, he stands before the door and knocks.

"If anyone hear my voice and open the door, to him will I go in and sup with him and he with me." Holy Communion is indeed an outward act. Actual men kneel by the altar, and each one individually receives the bread and wine. But it does not follow that Christ necessarily sups with every such person. No, *only he who hears Christ's voice, only he who opens the door,* i.e., the door of the heart. For the church door stands open for all, and one person can open the church door for another. But the door of the heart only the individual himself can open.

To him will I go in. It is true that at Holy Communion, according to the invitation, you do "come in," come to Christ. But communion is possible in truth, only when Christ comes to *you.*

I will sup with him and he with me. It is not so much we that have supper with Christ, but Christ who first has supper with us, and only then can we have supper with him. In other words, all is done solely through his grace, and not our choice. [X². A. 50.]

[1] Kierkegaard himself, however, wrote on April 22, 1838, " If Christ is to come and dwell with me, it must be, as it says in today's text in the Almanack: ' Christ comes in by closed doors.' " [II. A. 730; J 193.]

The Lord comes, even if we have to wait for him. He comes, even if we become old as Anna, gray as Simeon (that second Noah). But we must wait for him in *his house.* [II. A. 316; J 316.]

How glorious the call of the dragoons sounds! It is as if I already hear the beat of the hoofs as they charge. Listen! They are victorious! Their cry of victory resounds through the air!

And yet . . . what are all other calls compared with that which the Archangel shall one day blow: " Awake thou that sleepest, the Lord cometh." [III. A. 84.]

PRAYER

Lord, make thou our hearts thy temple wherein thou willest to dwell. Let every impure thought, every earthly desire, be found every morning, like the image of Dagon, broken in pieces at the feet of the Ark of the Covenant. Teach us to conquer flesh and blood, and let that be our " bloody sacrifice," so that with the apostle we may say, " I die daily." [II. A. 334.]

" Even so, come, Lord Jesus."